so simple
KNITS

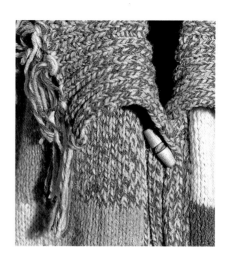

so simple
KNITS

A fabulous collection of
24 fashionable and fun designs

Hilary Mackin

CRE▲TIVE
HOMEOWNER®

INTRODUCTION

I have always had a keen interest in crafts.
I can still remember our knitting lessons at
elementary school and being the proud owner of my
first knitted dish cloth made in a thick cotton yarn. I
progressed onto scarves but don't think I actually
wore any of my efforts. I can remember pestering my
mother as to whether I was on a knit row or a purl
row, which is exactly what my daughter does to me
now. I was hooked. I grew up surrounded by people
who made their own clothes, knitted, embroidered,

and made their own soft furnishings. My granny,
mother, sister, and I used to have thrilling nights
sitting round the open fire, looking at knitting
magazines and choosing what to knit or make next.
We would long to go out to the local wool store to
choose the yarn. The excitement of knitting that first
row – even if it took a year to complete – was
overwhelming. Our hands were never idle. The
knitting project would appear while watching the
television, or any spare moment during the day.
Meanwhile, my father would be working on another
watercolor, away from the 'clickety clack' of the
knitting needles.

Knitting is such a rewarding craft and has such
tremendous scope. I have always been amazed at all
the different textures and color patterns that can be
achieved from one pair of knitting needles and a ball
of wool. Because every stitch pattern is based on the
simple knit one, purl one stitches, it never ceases to
amaze me that by adding variations, such as cabling,
you can produce such wonderful pieces of fabric.
Two garments of the same shape can look entirely
different by simply altering the yarn, stitch pattern, or
shade of color. Knitwear is comfortable and versatile
to wear, can look smart, casual, or glamorous, and is
suitable for all seasons.

I hope I have communicated some of my
enthusiasm for this wonderful craft. Whether you are
using this book as a complete beginner or as a
knowledgeable knitter, I'm sure there is plenty to
inspire you. Happy clicking!

BASIC INFORMATION

Equipment

Knitting requires very little equipment – all you need is a pair of needles and some yarn and you are ready to go. However, there are many types of yarn available and a wide range of needles to choose from, as well as some other equipment that you will find useful.

NEEDLES

Knitting needles are available in aluminum, plastic, and wood. The larger sizes are only made in plastic and wood, because they are lighter and easier to hold.

Standard needle sizes range from US 00 (2 mm) to US 15 (10 mm), although you will also find "fat" needles that can measure up to US 50 (25 mm). Generally, thick yarns are knitted using large needles and thinner yarns with small ones. The thicker the needle, the larger the stitch and the more quickly your work will progress. Needles also come in different lengths – choose ones that you find most comfortable to work with and that relate to the number of cast-on stitches.

Cable needles are short needles that are pointed at both ends. They are used for moving stitches from one position to another when working cables. Circular needles have two short needles that are each pointed and joined by a piece of flexible nylon which varies in length. They are much easier to handle than four double-pointed needles and are useful for neckbands or when picking up a large number of stitches around a front edge of the knitting. They are ideal for work which may be difficult to fit on a standard needle.

OTHER KNITTING ESSENTIALS

Crochet hooks
These are very useful for picking up dropped stitches and working edgings on finished garments, as well as for binding off, joining seams, and adding tassels.

Stitch holder
This keeps stitches that you are not using in place until you need them. You could also use a spare needle for this.

Tapestry needles
Blunt-ended needles with large eyes are used for sewing up items or sections because sharp needles may split the yarn and weaken it. The oversized eye allows for easy threading.

Tape measure
Use a good tape measure – ideally one that doesn't stretch, because accurate measurements are important when checking gauge.

Scissors
Have a sharp pair on hand for cutting lengths of yarn.

Row counter
This helps you keep track of stitches and rows completed.

Pins
Use long pins with large heads when securing pieces together so that they will not get lost in the knitting.

KNITTING NEEDLE CONVERSION TABLE

Metric	British	American
2 mm	14	00
2¼ mm	13	1
2¾ mm	12	2
3 mm	11	2/3
3¼ mm	10	3
3½ mm		4
3¾ mm	9	5
4 mm	8	6
4½ mm	7	7
5 mm	6	8
5½ mm	5	9
6 mm	4	10
6½ mm	3	10½
8 mm	0	11
9 mm	00	13
10 mm	000	15

Yarns

There is currently a huge selection of beautiful yarns available and choosing the right one can be daunting. You will find both natural and synthetic yarns as well as some synthetic mix yarns. Natural yarns, such as wool and cotton, are more expensive but they have a nicer hand and are easier to work with. Synthetic yarns tend to be stronger.

Wool is easily available, long lasting, and very warm. Merino sheep have the most abundant and highest quality yarn.

Cotton is strong, non-allergenic, and easy to wash but is less elastic than wool.

Mohair yarn comes from Angora goats. The long silky fibers make it very warm.

Angora is like mohair, but softer. It is made from the hair of the Angora goat or rabbit.

Alpaca is less fluffy than mohair and angora. It is made from the hair of a llamalike animal.

Cashmere is the most expensive and luxurious of yarns, made from the fine downy hair of a special breed of goat.

Chenille is a velvety yarn made of tufts of cotton and synthetic yarn.

CHOOSING YARNS

All the patterns in this book specify which yarns have been used. To ensure the item appears the same as in the pattern, you should use the yarn recommended in the pattern. If you cannot find the same yarn, choose one of a similar weight and type and knit a sample to check the gauge and appearance. When buying yarn, check the yarn label for the dye lot number and make sure you buy skeins with the same number. See page 126 for more detailed information about the yarns used in this book.

Getting started

GARTER STITCH

This is the simplest of all knitted stitches and is formed by working every row in the same stitch, either knit or purl, forming the same pebbly pattern on the front and the back, making it reversible. If every row is purled, however, you do not produce such a firm fabric.

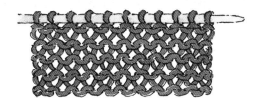

STOCKINETTE STITCH

This is the smoothest of all knitted stitches. It is formed by working alternate rows of knitted stitches and purled stitches. The smooth, knitted side is usually called the right side. When the pattern uses the purl side as the right side, it is referred to as reverse stockinette stitch.

SEED STITCH

This stitch forms a firmer fabric than stockinette stitch and is created by alternately working knit and purl stitches. Stitches that are knitted on one row will be knitted on the next row, and stitches that are purled on one row will be purled on the next row. For an odd number of stitches, the instructions will be as follows; K1, *p1, k1, rep from * to end. Repeat this row.

As this stitch does not curl at its ends, it is ideal for edges. It is also reversible.

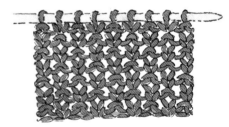

RIB STITCH

This stitch is formed by alternating knit and purl stitches across the same row. The knitted chain stitch forms a rib and the fabric 'shrinks' inward. It is particularly suitable for cuffs and necks and body edges as it forms a neat, stretchable finish. The stitch is usually worked on smaller needles than those used in the main body of the garment.

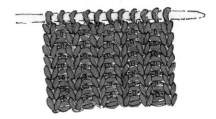

GAUGE

Making sure you have the correct gauge is extremely important, because it determines the shape and size of the knitted item. To make a gauge swatch, knit a sample slightly larger than a 4 in (10 cm) square using the same yarn, needles, and stitch pattern stated in the pattern. When finished, smooth out the sample on a flat surface, being careful not to stretch it. Using long pins, mark out the gauge measurement given in the pattern, usually 4 in (10 cm). To determine the stitch tension of the knitting, count the number of stitches between the pins. Remember to include any half stitches over the width of a garment; a half stitch left uncalculated may add several inches to the final width.

To determine the length of the knitted swatch, measure the number of rows. Place a rigid ruler or tape vertically along the swatch and count the number of rows to the inch. If the swatch is too wide, it means the knitting is too loose and a size smaller needle should be used. If too small, then the knitting is too tight and a larger needle should be used.

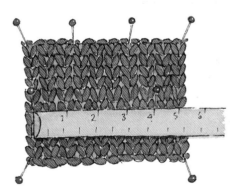

FOLLOWING A PATTERN

Knitting patterns are written in a language all of their own. Before starting to knit any pattern, always read it through so you are familiar with the terms.

Abbreviations are used for many of the repetitive words that occur in the instructions. See page 10 for a full list of abbreviations; any additional abbreviations will be given with each individual pattern.

Asterisks are used to indicate repetition of a sequence of stitches. For example: *k3, p1, rep from * to end. This means knit 3 stitches and purl 1 stitch to the end of the row.

ABBREVIATIONS

alt – alternate	psso – pass slipped st over
beg – beginning	rem – remain(ing)
cont – continue	rep – repeat
dec – decreas(e)(ing)	RH – right hand
foll – following	RS – right side
g st – garter stitch	sl 1 – slip one stitch
(every row knit)	sl1-k1-psso – slip one, knit
inc – increas(e)(ing)	one, pass slipped stitch over
k – knit	the knit one
k1b – knit one in back of loop	st(s) – stitch(es)
k2tog – knit two stitches	st st – stockinette stitch, (knit
together	row is RS, purl row is WS)
LH – left hand	tbl – through back of loop(s)
M1 – make one by picking up	tog – together
loop that lies between st	WS – wrong side
just worked and next st and	wyib – with yarn in back
working into the back of it	wyif – with yarn in front
p – purl	yb – yarn back
p1b – purl one in back of loop	yf – yarn forward
p2tog – purl two stitches	yo – yarn over needle
together	yrn – yarn round needle
patt – pattern	

Square brackets are used where a set of instructions needs to be worked a number of times. For example: [k3, p1] 4 times. This means that the stitches within the brackets are worked 4 times in total. Parentheses are used where instructions are given for multiple sizes; in the patterns, figures are given for the smallest size first, and the larger sizes follow in parentheses. Where the figure '0' appears in a set of parentheses, no stitches or rows are to be worked in that particular size.

The instruction 'alt' usually occurs during an instruction for shaping, for example: increase 1 stitch at the end of next and every alt row until there are 10 sts. This means that, counting the next row as row 1, the increase is worked on rows 1, 3, 5, 7 etc. until the required number of stitches is reached.

Care of yarns and garments

The correct aftercare of all knitted garments is extremely important if they are to retain their original texture and shape. Many of the yarns available today are machine-washable, and the yarn label will clearly indicate where this is applicable. If in any doubt, handwash in warm soapy water and lay flat to dry. Check the yarn label to see whether the yarn can be dry cleaned.

When washing by hand, handle the knitting carefully and never lift the garment by the shoulders, because the weight of the wet wool will drag the knitting out of shape. Squeeze out excess moisture gently without wringing. Support the overall weight with both hands and rinse thoroughly before drying to avoid matting.

Never tumble dry a knitted garment. Knitting should be laid out flat on a suitable surface and dried away from direct heat. Spread the knitting out gently on a towel, and smooth out any creases. Leave until completely dry and then place over a line for final airing. Never hang knitting to drip dry. The weight of the wet fabric will pull the garment out of shape.

If a garment is properly dried, it should not need pressing. If it does, check the instructions on the yarn label. Some yarns may need steaming or pressing over a damp cloth. Never use a heavy hand when pressing knitted garments because this could distort the shape badly, and never press ribbing.

Some yarns are prone to pilling during wear. This means that loose fibers gather into balls of fluff on the surface of the knitting. These can either be picked off, or combed away. Alternativly, you could go over the surface with a strip of adhesive tape, sticky side down. Special implements can be bought for this purpose. If a snag occurs, never cut it off; instead, take a blunt needle and push the snag through to the wrong side of the work. Gently tighten the yarn until the stitch is the right size and then knot the end on the wrong side.

Basic techniques

INCREASING AND DECREASING

Garments are most commonly shaped by increasing or decreasing the number of stitches in a row. There are many ways of increasing and decreasing the number of stitches, and each will create a different appearance.

Increases and decreases are usually worked in pairs at each end of the row on the symmetrical pieces (back, sleeves, etc) to give a balanced shape.

Yarn over increase

To make the yarn over increase in a knit row, bring the yarn to the front, take it over the right-hand needle, and knit the stitch. The complete increase creates a visible hole and is often used in lace patterns. The increase is abbreviated in knitting patterns as yf (yarn forward).

In a purl row, take the yarn over the right-hand needle to the back of the work, then under the needle to the front. The abbreviation is yrn (yarn round needle).

Make 1 increase

Lift the yarn lying between the stitch just worked and the next stitch and place it on the left-hand needle, then knit (or purl) into the back of this loop. This increase is abbreviated as M1 (make 1).

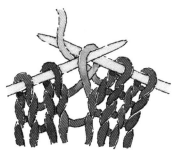

Slip stitch decrease

Slip the next stitch onto the right-hand needle without knitting it, then knit the next stitch. Lift the slipped stitch over the knitted stitch and drop it off the needle. This decrease is abbreviated as sl 1, k1, psso (on right side) and sl 1, p1, psso (on wrong side).

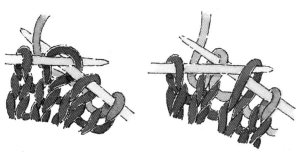

Working two stitches together

This decrease is worked simply by inserting the right-hand needle through two stitches instead of one and then knitting them together as one stitch. On a purl row, insert the needle purlwise through the two stitches and purl in the usual way. This decrease is abbreviated as k2tog (right side) or p2tog (wrong side).

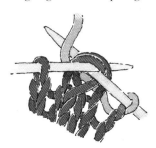

CHANGING SHADE

To join in a new shade at the start of a row, insert the needle into the first stitch and, using the new shade, make a loop over the right-hand needle. Pull through to complete the stitch and continue to the end of the row. Carry the yarn up the side of the work for narrow stripes, but break it off and rejoin it for wider stripes.

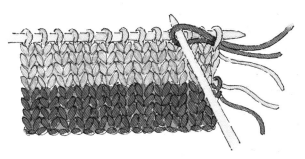

Where shades are worked in blocks, it is best to use a separate ball of yarn for each section. Twist the yarns over each other at the junction of each shade change to avoid forming a hole. When the shade change occurs in vertical lines, cross the yarns on both knit and purl rows. When the shade change is on a slanting line, the yarns need to be crossed on alternate rows.

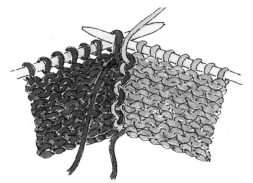

MAKING HORIZONTAL BUTTONHOLES

These may be worked on the main fabric or on a separate narrow band.

Work to the position of the buttonhole and bind off the number of stitches required for the width of the button and knit to the end of the row. Work to within one stitch of the bound-off stitches and knit twice into it. Then cast on one stitch less than was bound off and work to the end of the row.

Once the garment is complete, you can finish off the buttonhole by working round it in buttonhole stitch.

FINISHING GARMENTS

Even the simplest garments require neat and careful finishing, so it is worth spending some time at the final stages for professional looking garments.

Before you begin joining pieces together, weave in any loose ends of yarn into a seam edge. Cover the pieces with a damp cloth and press gently with a steam iron – this will make them easier to join.

Joining seams

There are various ways of sewing knitted pieces together, but the garments in this book use the backstitch seam method. Use a blunt-ended needle.

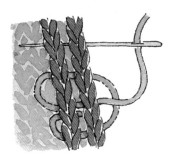

Place the pieces to be joined together with their right sides facing inward, ensuring that the stitches and rows are aligned. Sewing into the center of each stitch, bring the needle out one stitch in from the edge, insert the needle one stitch back, and bring the needle out one stitch ahead of the emerging thread. Sew ¼ in (a few mm) in from the edge of the knitting.

Joining sleeves

The top of the sleeve and the armhole into which it is set can often be different shapes, so care needs to be taken when inserting the sleeves. One approach is to use marker pins. Once the shoulder seams have been joined, fold the sleeve in half lengthwise and use pins to mark the center of the top of the sleeve and the midway points between the center and the underarm.

On the main body of the garment, use pins to mark the center of the shoulder join and midway points from that point and the underarm. With right sides together and edges even, pin the sleeve into the armhole, matching up the marker pins. Using a backstitch seam, sew the sleeve seam on the inside.

Collars

Collars can either be knitted in by first picking up stitches around the neck edge or made separately and sewn on.

For a picked-up collar, join one shoulder as indicated on the pattern. Divide the neck edge into sections and mark with pins to space the picked-up stitches evenly, then calculate how many stitches will be needed for each section. When working a non-reversible stitch such as stockinette stitch, remember to pick up the stitches from the correct side to ensure that the pattern is on the right side when the collar is turned over.

For a sewn-on collar, divide the neck edge and the inner collar edge into the same number of equal sections and mark them with a pin. With the right side of the collar facing the wrong side of the garment, pin the two edges together and sew.

Zippers

Always insert an open-ended zipper with the fastener closed to ensure that both sides match.

Pin the zipper in position, taking care not to stretch the knitting. Use an ordinary sewing needle and matching thread. With the right side of the work facing, sew in the zipper with a back-stitch seam, keeping as close to the knitted edge as possible. Always work from top to bottom and take care not to cover the zipper teeth. Tack down the zipper edges on the inside afterward.

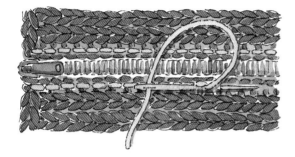

Decorative edges

These may be used to trim garments. They can be made separately and sewn on afterward or knitted as part of the garment. Knit a length as indicated on the pattern. Then, with right side of edging to right side of garment, divide into equal sections and pin. Sew in position using a back stitch. Allow extra ease for any curves on the main garment, so that the edging lies flat after sewing.

Making tassels

Cut out a piece of stiff card the same length that you want the tassel to be. Wind yarn around the card to the required thickness. Thread a needle with yarn and insert and pull it under the strands at the top of the card. Tie securely, leaving a long end. Using a sharp pair of scissors, cut through the yarn at the opposite end of the card. Wind the long end of yarn around the tassel several times about ¾ in (1.5 cm) from the top and secure by pushing the needle up through the middle of the tassel.

Fringing

Cut the yarn into the required lengths – just over twice the required finished length of the fringe. Fold in half and, with the wrong side of the fabric facing you, draw a loop through the edge stitch using a crochet hook. Then draw the loose ends of the strands through this loop and pull down tightly to form a knot. Repeat at regular intervals.

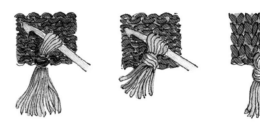

Sewn-on pockets

Use a slip stitch seam to apply the pocket, taking care to keep the line of the pocket and main fabric straight. A useful tip is to use a fine knitting needle, pointed at both ends, to pick up every alternate stitch along the line of the main fabric, then to catch one stitch from the edge of the pocket and one stitch from the needle alternately. Make sure that the lower edge of the pocket lies in a straight line across a row of the main fabric.

ADAPTING PATTERNS

Sometimes it may be necessary to alter a pattern to suit your own body measurements. Working with the gauge quoted on the pattern, calculate the amendments necessary to the stitches and rows and mark the alterations on the pattern.

CLASSIC

In this chapter you will find timeless classics knitted in wonderful modern yarns, with features, such as loop stitch collars, fringing, and easy stitches. Wear them with jeans for a casual look to be comfortably smart. There are ideas here for classic styling that would be ideal for any place or occasion – the office, out to lunch, shopping, or days out. Win admiring glances when you wear any of the easy and quick-to-knit coats. The shawl-collared coat on page 26 looks fabulous when paired with the striped sweater on page 32 – the colors complement each other perfectly.

This stylish coat is knitted in stockinette stitch with garter stitch borders. Its soft drape and classic style make it suited to any occasion.

LONG ASYMMETRICAL COAT

✋ *Although this is a very easy garment to knit, the asymmetrical shaping requires accurate row counting.*

HELPFUL HINT

- To make sure the front sections are even, lay the garment out before sewing the front band in position. Sew with a back stitch, stretching the front bands slightly around the front edges above button fastenings.

MEASUREMENTS

To fit bust

32	34	36	38	40	42	in
81	86	91	97	102	107	cm

Actual width

45¼	47¼	49½	51¼	53¼	55¼	in
115	120	125	130	135	140	cm

Actual length

30½	39½	40	41	41¾	43	in
98	100	102	104	106	109	cm

Actual sleeve seam

17	18	18	18	18	18½	in
43	46	46	46	46	47	cm

In the instructions, figures are given for the smallest size first; larger sizes follow in parentheses. Where only one set of figures is given, this applies to all sizes.

MATERIALS

- 12 (13:14:15:16:17) × 100 g balls of Rowan Big Wool in Tremble 035 (MC)
- 3 × 100 g balls of Rowan Yorkshire Tweed Chunky in Stout 554 (C)
- Pair each of US 10½ (6½ mm) and US 17 (12¾ mm) needles
- Buckle, 2½ in (6 cm) in diameter
- Button

GAUGE

8 sts and 11 rows to 4 in (10 cm) measured over stockinette stitch using MC and US 17 (12¾ mm) needles.

ABBREVIATIONS

See page 10.

COAT

BACK

With US 10½ (6½ mm) needles and C, cast on 65 (68:71:73:76:79) sts and knit 7 rows.
Dec row: (k1, k2tog) 6 (6:7:6:6:7) times, (k2, k2tog) 7 (7:7:9:9:9) times, (k1, k2tog) 6 (7:7:6:7:7) times, k1.
[46 (48:50:52:54:56) sts.]
Change to US 17 (12¾ mm) needles and MC.
Cont in st st, beg with a knit row, work 104 (106:108:110:112:116) rows, ending with a WS row.
Work measures approximately 38½ (39½:40:41:41¾:43) in (98 (100:102:104:106:109) cm) from beg.

Shape shoulder

Bind off 5 (5:5:5:6:6) sts at beg of the next 2 rows, 5 (5:6:6:6:6) sts on the next 2 rows, 5 (6:6:6:6:7) sts on the next 2 rows. Bind off rem 16 (16:16:18:18:18) sts.

LEFT FRONT

With US 10½ (6½ mm) needles and C, cast on 33 (34:35:37:38:39) sts and knit 7 rows.

Dec row: K2 (3:3:3:3:4), (k2tog, k1) 9 (9:9:10:10:10) times, k2tog, k2 (2:3:2:3:3). [23 (24:25:26:27:28) sts.]

Change to US 17 (12¾ mm) needles and MC. Cont in st st beg with a knit row. Work 5 (7:9: 5:7:9) rows, then inc 1 st at beg (front edge) on the next and at this same edge every 8th row 0 (0:0:3:3:3) times [24 (25:26:30:31:32) sts], then every 6th row 9 (9:9:6:6:6) times. [33 (34:35:36:37:38) sts.] Work 6 rows. Place a marker at front edge on the last row. Dec 1 st at front edge on the next and 12 (12:12:13:13:13) foll alt rows, then every 4th row 5 times. [15 (16:17:17:18:19) sts.] Work 3 (3:5:3:3:5) rows, ending with a WS row.

Shape shoulder

Bind off 5 (5:5:5:6:6) sts at beg of the next row, 5 (5:6:6:6:6) sts on the foll alt row. Work 1 row. Bind off rem 5 (6:6:6:6:7) sts.

RIGHT FRONT

Work as given for Left Front, reversing shapings.

SLEEVES (MAKE 2)

With US 10½ (6½ mm) needles and C, cast on 38 (38:41:41:44:44) sts and knit 7 rows.

Dec row: K2, (k1, k2tog) 11 (11:12:12:13:13) times, k3. [27 (27:29:29:31:31) sts.]

Change to US 17 (12¾ mm) needles and MC. Cont in st st beg with a knit row, at the same time inc 1 st at both ends of the 13th (13th: 9th:9th:7th:7th) row and every 14th (14th: 10th:10th:8th:8th) row 2 (2:3:3:4:4) times. [33 (33:37:37:41:41) sts.] Cont straight until Sleeve measures 43 (43:46:46:46:47) cm (17 (18:18:18:18:18½) in) from beg, ending with a WS row.

Shape sleeve top

Bind off 6 (6:7:7:8:8) sts at beg of the next 4 rows. Bind off rem 9 sts.

POCKETS (MAKE 2)

With US 10½ (6½ mm) needles and C, cast on 20 sts. Knit 1 row.

Dec row: K1, (k1, k2tog) 6 times, k1. [14 sts.]

Change to US 17 (12¾ mm) needles and MC. Cont in st st beg with a knit row. Work 15 rows.

Inc row: WS. P1, (p2, M1) 6 times, p1. [20 sts.]

Change to US 10½ (6½ mm) needles and C. Knit 8 rows. Bind off.

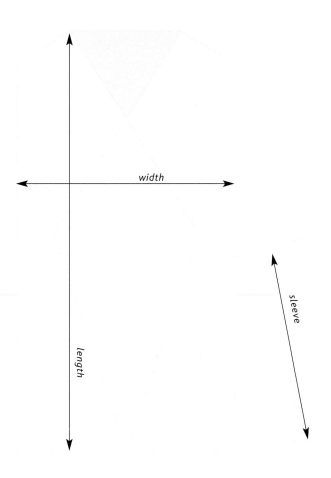

POCKET SIDES (MAKE 2)

With right side facing, US 10½ (6½ mm) needles and C, knit up 20 sts along one side edge of pocket. Knit 1 row. Bind off. Rep on other side.

TIES

Right front

With US 10½ (6½ mm) needles and C, cast on 26 sts. Knit 7 rows. Bind off.

Left front

With US 10½ (6½ mm) needles and C, cast on 10 sts. Knit 7 rows. Bind off.

TO FINISH

Join shoulders.

Front band

With US 10½ (6½ mm) needles and C, cast on 7 sts.

Next row: Sl 1, k5, k1b.

Rep this row until band fits all round fronts and back neck edge. Bind off.

Sew on Front Band.

Attach Right Front Tie, positioning top corner to marker on Right Front, and under Front Band.

Position top of Left Front Tie, 4 (4½:4¾:5:5½:6) in (10 (11:12:13:14:15) cm) in from side seam in line with marker on Left Front, sew down top and bottom for 1¼ in

(3 cm) and short end of Tie nearest side seam. To cover the buckle, wrap the same yarn as used for the ties around the buckle and secure with a buttonhole stitch. Wrap other end of tie around inner stem of Buckle and secure. Sew a loop to edge of Front Band on Left Front so that the top of loop lies at marker. Sew a button to wrong side of Right Front to correspond with loop.

Sew pockets neatly to Fronts, positioning the bottom of the pocket 13 (13¾:14:15:15¾:16½) in (33 (35:36:38:40:42) cm) up from cast-on edge and 1¼ in (3 cm) in from side seam. Fold sleeves in half lengthwise, place folds to shoulder seams, and sew sleeves in position approximately 8¾ (8¾:9½:9½:9¾:9¾) in (22 (22:24:24:25:25) cm) from top of shoulder. Join side and sleeve seams.

Pin out garment to the measurement given on page 16. Cover with damp cloths and leave until dry.

Although this is a large garment, it can be knitted very quickly. The attractive basketweave fabric is really easy to create and the large sailor collar and tassels are the perfect details. To top it all, you can knit a matching beret.

BASKETWEAVE COAT AND HAT

Some experience is needed to create the basketweave fabric.

This garment requires neat finishing.

MEASUREMENTS

To fit bust

32–34	36–38	40–42	44–46	48–50	in
81–86	91–97	102–107	112–117	122–127	cm

Actual width

43½	48½	51¼	56¼	59	in
110	123	130	143	150	cm

Actual length

40	42	44	46	48	in
102	107	112	117	122	cm

Actual sleeve seam

16½	16½	16½	17½	17½	in
42	42	42	44	44	cm

In the instructions, figures are given for the smallest size first; larger sizes follow in parentheses. Where only one set of figures is given, this applies to all sizes.

MATERIALS

For the coat

- 18 (19:20:21:22) × 100 g balls of Sirdar Bigga in Blue Suede 694
- Pair of US 19 (15 mm) needles
- Stitch holders
- 3 buttons

For the hat

- 2 × 100 g balls of Sirdar Bigga in Blue Suede 694
- Pair of US 19 (15 mm) needles

GAUGE

6 sts and 9 rows to 4 in (10 cm) measured over stockinette stitch using US 19 (15 mm) needles.

ABBREVIATIONS

See page 10.

COAT

BACK

With US 19 (15 mm) needles cast on 33 (37:39:43:45) sts.

Row 1: RS. *K1, p1; rep from * to last st, k1.

Row 2: *P1, k1; rep from * to last st, p1.

These 2 rows form the rib. Work 4 more rows in rib. Cont in main patt as follows:

Row 1: RS. Knit.

Row 2: K3 (5:2:4:5), *p3, k5; rep from * to last 6 (8:5:7:8) sts, p3, k3 (5:2:4:5).

Row 3: P3 (5:2:4:5), *k3, p5; rep from * to last 6 (8:5:7:8) sts, k3, p3 (5:2:4:5).

Row 4: As Row 2.

Row 5: Knit.

Row 6: P2 (0:1:3:0), k5 (1:5:5:1), *p3, k5; rep from * to last 10 (4:9:11:4) sts, p3, k5 (1:5:5:1), p2 (0:1:3:0).

Row 7: K2 (0:1:3:0), p5 (1:5:5:1), *k3, p5; rep from * to last 10 (4:9:11:4) sts, k3, p5 (1:5:5:1), k2 (0:1:3:0).

Row 8: As Row 6.

These 8 rows form the main patt and are repeated throughout.

HELPFUL HINT

When buying yarn, check the yarn label for the dye lot number. Different dye lot numbers mean that the shades may differ slightly, so make sure you buy the correct number of skeins with the same dye lot number – especially when you are picking up and knitting a large project such as this one.

Cont in patt until work measures 40 (42:44:46:48) in (102 (107:112:117:122) cm) from beg, ending with a WS row.

Shape shoulders

Bind off 6 (7:7:8:8) sts at beg of the next 2 rows. [21 (23:25:27:29) sts.]
Bind off 6 (7:8:8:9) sts at beg of the next 2 rows. Bind off rem 9 (9:9:11:11) sts.

POCKET LININGS (MAKE 2)

With US 19 (15 mm) needles and using the thumb method, cast on 11 sts. Work 16 rows in st st beg with a knit row. Leave sts on a st holder.

LEFT FRONT

With US 19 (15 mm) needles cast on 20 (22:24:26:28) sts and work 6 rows in rib as follows:

Row 1: RS. *K1, p1; rep from * to last 2 sts, k1, k1b.

Row 2: Sl 1, *p1, k1; rep from * to last st, p1. Work 4 more rows in rib.
Cont in main patt as follows:

Row 1: RS. Knit to the last 4 sts, k1, p1, k1, k1b (these last 4 sts form the front band).

Row 2: Sl 1, p1, k1, p1 (these 4 sts form the front band), p0 (0:2:2:3), k2 (2:5:5:5), p3, k5, p3, k3 (5:2:4:5).

Row 3: P3 (5:2:4:5), k3, p5, k3, p2 (2:5:5:5), k0 (0:2:2:3), k1, p1, k1, k1b.

Row 4: As Row 2.

Row 5: Knit to the last 4 sts, k1, p1, k1, k1b.

Row 6: Sl 1, p1, k1, p1, k0 (0:3:3:4), p1 (1:3:3:3), k5, p3, k5, p2 (3:1:3:3), k0 (1:0:0:1).

Row 7: P0 (3:0:0:1), k2 (3:1:3:3), p5, k3, p5, k1 (1:3:3:3), p0 (0:3:3:4), k1, p1, k1, k1b.

Row 8: As Row 6.
Cont straight in patt as now set until work measures 21 (23:24½:26:27½) in (53 (58:62:66:70) cm) from beg, ending with a WS row.

Place pocket

Patt 3 (4:5:6:7), slip the next 11 sts on a st holder and patt across 11 sts from one st holder for pocket lining, patt 2 (3:4:5:6), k1, p1, k1, k1b.
Cont straight in patt on these sts until Front measures 22 (24:26:28:30) rows shorter than Back to beg of shoulder shaping, ending with a WS row. **

Work rib for collar

Row 1: Patt to last 7 sts, work 2tog, k1, M1, rib to end.

Row 2: Sl 1, rib 4, M1, p1, patt to end.

Row 3: Patt to last 9 sts, work 2tog, k1, M1, rib to end.

Row 4: Sl 1, rib 6, M1, p1, patt to end.

Row 5: Patt to last 11 sts, work 2tog, k1, M1, rib to end.

Row 6: Sl 1, rib 8, M1, p1, patt to end.

Row 7: Patt to last 13 sts, work 2tog, k1, M1, rib to end.

Row 8: Sl 1, rib 10, M1, p1, patt to end.

Row 9: Patt to last 15 sts, work 2tog, k1, M1, rib to end.

Row 10: Sl 1, rib 12, M1, p1, patt to end.
[25 (27:29:31:33) sts.]

2nd, 3rd, 4th, and 5th sizes

Row 11: Patt to last 17 sts, work 2tog, k1, M1, rib to end.

Row 12: Sl 1, rib 14, M1, p1, patt to end.
[(28:30:32:34) sts.]

3rd, 4th, and 5th sizes

Row 13: Patt to last 19 sts, work 2tog, k1, M1, rib to end.

Row 14: Sl 1, rib 16, M1, p1, patt to end.
[(31:33:35) sts.]

4th and 5th sizes

Row 15: Patt to last 21 sts, work 2tog, k1, M1, rib to end.

Row 16: Sl 1, rib 18, M1, p1, patt to end.
[(34:36) sts.]

5th size

Row 17: Patt to last 23 sts, work 2tog, k1, M1, rib to end.

Row 18: Sl 1, rib 20, M1, p1, patt to end.
[37 sts.]

All sizes

Cont straight in patt as now set until work measures same as Back to beg of shoulder shaping, ending with a WS row.

Shape shoulder

Bind off 6 (7:7:8:8) sts at beg of the next row [19 (21:24:26:29) sts], 6 (7:8:8:9) sts on the foll alt row ending with a RS row. Leave rem 13 (14:16:18:20) sts on a st holder.

Place markers for 3 buttons on front band, the first to come 16 (17½:19:20½:22) in (41 (44:48:52:56) cm) up from cast-on edge, the last 1¼ in (3 cm) down from beg of rib for collar and the remaining spaced evenly between.

RIGHT FRONT

With US 19 (15 mm) needles cast on 20 (22:24:26:28) sts and work 6 rows in rib as follows:

Row 1: RS. Sl 1, *k1, p1; rep from * to last st, k1.

Row 2: *P1, k1; rep from * to last 2 sts, p1, k1b.

Cont in main patt placing patt as follows:

Row 1: Sl 1, k1, p1, k1, knit to end.

Row 2: K3 (5:2:4:5), p3, k5, p3, k2 (2:5:5:5), p0 (0:2:2:3), p1, k1, p1, k1b.

Row 3: Sl 1, k1, p1, k1, k0 (0:2:2:3), p2 (2:5:5:5), k3, p5, k3, p3 (5:2:4:5).

Row 4: As Row 2.

Row 5: Sl 1, k1, p1, k1, knit to end.

Row 6: K0 (1:0:0:1), p2 (3:1:3:3), k5, p3, k5, p1 (1:3:3:3), k0 (0:3:3:4), p1, k1, p1, k1b.

Row 7: Sl 1, k1, p1, k1, p0 (0:3:3:4), k1 (1:3:3:3), p5, k3, p5, k2 (3:1:3:3), p0 (1:0:0:1).

Row 8: As Row 6.

Cont straight in patt as now set making buttonholes in front band to correspond with markers on Left Front as follows:

Buttonhole row – right side
Sl 1, k1, yo, k2tog, patt to end.
Place pocket when work measures 21 (23:24½:26:27½) in (53 (58:62:66:70) cm) from beg, ending with a WS row.

Place pocket
Next row: Sl 1, k1, p1, k1, patt 2 (3:4:5:6), sl the next 11 sts on a st holder and patt across 11 sts from rem pocket st holder, patt rem 3 (4:5:6:7) sts.
Cont straight in patt on these sts working as given for Left Front to **.

Work rib for collar
Row 1: RS. Sl 1, rib 3, M1, k1, work 2tog, patt to end.
Row 2: Patt to last 6 sts, p1, M1, rib 4, k1b.
Complete as   for Left Front, reversing shapings.

SLEEVES (MAKE 2)
With US 19 (15 mm) needles cast on 21 (21:23:23:25) sts and work 6 rows in rib as given for Back.
Cont in main patt placing patt as follows:
Row 1: RS. Knit.

Row 2: K1 (1:2:2:3), (p3, k5) twice, p3, k1 (1:2:2:3).
Row 3: P1 (1:2:2:3), (k3, p5) twice, k3, p1 (1:2:2:3).
Cont in patt as given for Back as now set, at the same time inc 1 st at both ends of the 13th (13th:7th:7th:7th) row, then every 13th (13th: 8th:8th:7th) row 1 (1:2:2:3) time(s).
[25 (25:29:29:33) sts.]
Cont straight in patt until Sleeve measures 16½ (16½:16½:17½:17½) in (42 (42:42:44:44) cm) from beg, ending with a WS row.

Shape sleeve top
Bind off 5 (5:6:6:6) sts at beg of the next 2 rows, [15 (15:17:17:21) sts], 5 (5:6:6:7) sts at beg of the next 2 rows. Bind off rem 5 (5:5:5:7) sts.

BACK COLLAR
Join shoulders.
Next row: Beg at front edge st on Right Front Collar, sl 1, rib 12 (13:15:17:19), M1, pick up and knit 9 (9:9:11:11) sts from back neck, starting at neck edge on Left Front Collar, M1, rib 12 (13:15:17:19), k1b.
[37 (39:43:49:53) sts.]
Cont in rib until Back Collar measures 11¾ in (30 cm), ending with a WS row. Bind off ribwise.

POCKET BORDERS (MAKE 2)
With RS facing and US 19 (15 mm) needles,

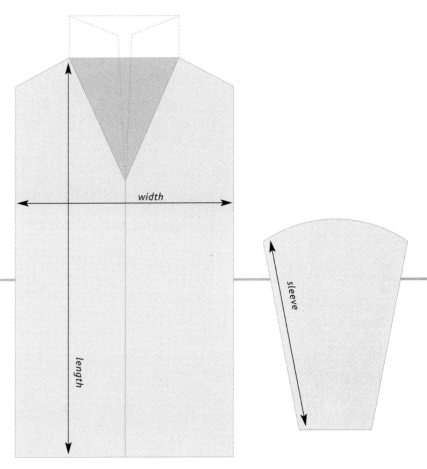

rib across 11 sts from one pocket top. Rib 2 more rows. Bind off ribwise.

TO FINISH

Sew pocket linings and borders in position. Sew sleeves in position approximately 8¼ (8¼:9½:9½:11) in (21 (21:24:24:28) cm) from top of shoulder. Join side and sleeve seams. For each tassel, cut 3 strands of yarn each approximately 11 in (28 cm), see Making Tassels, page 13. Tie in tassels to bind-off edge on Collar approximately 4 sts apart. Trim as required so that each tassel measures 4¾ in (12 cm). Sew on buttons.

Cover with a damp cloth and leave until dry.

HAT

With US 19 (15 mm) needles, cast on 31 sts.
Row 1: RS. *P1, k1; rep from * to last st, p1.
Row 2: *K1, p1; rep from * to last st, k1.
Row 3: As row 1.
Inc row: K3, *M1, k2; rep from * 13 times, M1, k2. [45 sts.]
Cont in patt as follows:
Row 1: RS. Knit.
Row 2: K5, *p3, k5; rep from * to end.
Row 3: P5, *k3, p5; rep from * to end.
Row 4: As Row 2.
Row 5: Knit.
Row 6: K1, *p3, k5; rep from * end last rep k1.
Row 7: P1, *k3, p5; rep from * end last rep p1.

Row 8: As Row 6.
Knit 2 rows.

Shape crown

Row 1 dec: RS. *Sl 1, k1, psso, k1, k2tog, k4; rep from * 5 times. [35 sts.]
Purl 1 row.
Row 2 dec: *Sl 1, k1, psso, k1, k2tog, k2; rep from * 5 times. [25 sts.]
Purl 1 row.
Row 3 dec: *Sl 1, k1, psso, k1, k2tog; rep from * 5 times. [15 sts.]
Purl 1 row.
Row 4 dec: *K2tog; rep from * 7 times, k1. [8 sts.]
Purl 1 row.
Row 5 dec: *K2tog; rep from * 4 times. [4 sts.]
Break yarn and thread through sts, pull up tightly, and secure.
Join back seam.
Make a tassel as given for Collar and tie in to center of crown (see Making Tassels, page 13).

This interesting yarn, together with an easy slip stitch pattern, gives extra appeal to this long line coat, which is perfect for wearing over a pair of casual pants for a warm yet elegant look.

LONG SHAWL-COLLARED COAT

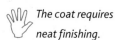 **MEDIUM**

The slip stitch pattern used to make this coat is very easy to work.

Some experience is needed to do the shaping and collar on this garment.

The coat requires neat finishing.

MEASUREMENTS
To fit bust

32	34	36	38	40	in
81	86	91	97	102	cm

Actual width

37½	39½	41	44½	46	in
95	100	104	113	117	cm

Actual length

35½	35½	36¼	36¼	37	in
90	90	92	92	94	cm

Actual sleeve seam
18 in (46 cm)

In the instructions, figures are given for the smallest size first; larger sizes follow in parentheses. Where only one set of figures is given, this applies to all sizes.

MATERIALS
- 14 (14:15:15:16) × 100 g balls of Rowan Ribbon Twist in Ribble 111
- Pair of US 17 (12¾ mm) needles
- Stitch holders
- 3 buttons

GAUGE
9 sts and 11 rows to 4 in (10 cm) measured over pattern using US 17 (12¾ mm) needles.

ABBREVIATIONS
See page 10.

COAT

BACK
With US 17 (12¾ mm) needles cast on 51 (55:59:63:67) sts.
Foundation row: WS. *K3, p1; rep from * to last 3 sts, k3.
Row 1: *P3, k1 winding yarn twice round needle; rep from * to last 3 sts, p3.
Row 2: *K3, sl 1 purlwise wyif and dropping extra loop, yb; rep from * to last 3 sts, k3.
Rows 1 and 2 form the patt. Cont in patt dec 1 st at each end of the 17th row, then every 8th (8th:6th:6th:6th) row 5 (2:6:6:4) times [39 (49:45:49:57) sts], then every 0 (6th:4th:4th:4th) row 0 (4:1:1:4) time(s) [39 (41:43:47:49) sts], then inc 1 st at each end of the next and foll 6th row. [43 (45:47:51:53) sts.]
Work 10 rows straight, ending with a WS row. [74 rows – work measures approximately 26½ in (67 cm) from beg.]

Shape armholes
Bind off 2 (2:3:3:4) sts at beg of the next 2 rows [39 (41:41:45:45) sts], then dec 1 st at each end of the next 3 rows [33 (35:35:39:39) sts], then on the 2 foll alt

rows [29 (31:31:35:35) sts]. Work a further 15 (15:17:17:19) patt rows, ending with a WS row.

Shape shoulders and back neck

Bind off 4 (4:4:5:5) sts at beg of the next row, work in patt until there are 5 (6:6:6:6) sts on RH needle after bind-off, turn, and leave rem sts on a st holder. Work on these sts for first side.

Dec 1 st at neck edge on the next row. Bind off rem 4 (5:5:5:5) sts.

With RS facing, bind off the center 11 (11:11:13:13) sts and work in patt to end. Complete this side to match first side, reversing shapings.

POCKET LININGS (MAKE 2)

With US 17 (12¾ mm) needles, cast on 11 sts. Cont in st st beg with a knit row. Work 14 rows and leave on a st holder.

LEFT FRONT

With US 17 (12¾ mm) needles cast on 30 (34:36:38:40) sts.

Cont in patt as follows:

Foundation row: WS. (P1, k1) 3 times, p1, k3 (3:5:3:5), p1, *k3, p1; rep from * to last 3 sts, k3.

Row 1: *P3, k1 winding yarn twice round needle; rep from * to last 10 (10:12:10:12) sts, p3 (3:5:3:5), (k1, p1) 3 times, k1.

Row 2: (P1, k1) 3 times, p1, k3 (3:5:3:5), p1, *k3, sl 1 purlwise wyif and dropping extra loop, yb; rep from * to last 3 sts, k3.

Cont in patt as Back, dec 1 st at side edge on the 17th row, then every 8th (8th:6th:6th:6th) row 3 (2:4:4:4) times [26 (31:31:33:35) sts], then every 0 (6th:0:0:4th) row 0 (2:0:0:1) time(s). [26 (29:31:33:34) sts]. Work 5 (1:5:5:1) rows, ending with WS row.

Place pocket

Next row: Patt 0 (0:2:2:0) tog, patt 4 (5:4:5:8) sts, rib across next 11 sts for pocket top, turn and work 2 rows in rib on these 11 sts, bind off these 11 sts. Break yarn. With RS facing, rejoin yarn to one pocket lining, cont in patt across these sts, then patt 4 (6:7:7:8), rib 7. [26 (29:30:32:34) sts.]

Work 1 (3:5:5:1) rows. Dec 1 st at side edge on the next and 1 (1:1:1:2) foll 8th (6th:4th:4th:4th) row [24 (27:28:30:31) sts], then inc 1 st at side edge on the next and foll 6th row. [26 (29:30:32:33) sts.]

Work 4 rows straight, ending with a WS row. Place marker at front edge on last row. ***

Shape neck and collar

Row 1: Patt to last 10 sts, patt 3tog, M1, rib to end. [25 (28:29:31:32) sts.]

Row 2: Rib 8, patt to end.

Row 3: Patt to last 8 sts, M1, rib to end. [26 (29:30:32:33) sts.]

This simple crew neck style sweater is worked in stockinette stitch – one of the easiest stitches for creating knitted fabric. Worked here in pretty pastel colors in a stripe design, the sweater can be worn with pants or a skirt.

STRIPED SWEATER

★ ☆ ☆ BEGINNER

🖐 *This garment is very easy to knit, but take care not to pull the yarn too tightly when carrying the colors up the side of the work.*

MEASUREMENTS
To fit bust

32	34	36	38	40	in
81	86	91	97	102	cm

Actual width

34	36	38	40	42½	in
86	91	97	102	108	cm

Actual length

21	21	21¼	21½	22	in
53	53	54	55	56	cm

Actual sleeve seam
18 in (46 cm)

In the instructions, figures are given for the smallest size first; larger sizes follow in parentheses. Where only one set of figures is given, this applies to all sizes.

MATERIALS
- 4 (5:5:6:7) × 50 g balls of Rowan Cotton Glace in Stout 814 (A)
- 3 (4:4:5:6) × 50 g balls of Rowan Cotton Glace in Pier 809 (B)
- 3 (3:3:4:4) × 50 g balls of Rowan Cotton Glace in Zeal 813 (C)
- 2 (2:2:3:3) × 50 g balls of Rowan Cotton Glace in Splendor 810 (D)
- Pair each of US 2/3 (3 mm) and US 5 (3¾ mm) needles
- Stitch holders

GAUGE
22 sts and 30 rows to 4 in (10 cm) measured over stockinette stitch using US 5 (3¾ mm) needles.

ABBREVIATIONS
See page 10.

STRIPED SWEATER

Striped pattern
Work 8 rows in A, 6 rows in B, 4 rows in C, 2 rows in D, 4 rows in C, 6 rows in B, 8 rows in A, 2 rows in D, 2 rows in C, 2 rows in D. These 44 rows form the patt.

BACK
With US 2/3 (3 mm) needles and A cast on 95 (101:107:113:119) sts and knit 9 rows. Change to US 5 (3¾ mm) needles. Cont in st st beg with a knit row, working Stripe Sequence patt as above throughout, at the same time dec 1 st at each end of every 5th row 5 times. [85 (91:97:103:109) sts.]
Work 9 rows, then inc 1 st at each end of the next then every 10th row 4 times. [95 (101:107:113:119) sts.]
Work 19 rows, ending with a 6th patt row.

Shape armholes
Bind off 6 (7:8:8:9) sts at beg of the next 2 rows [83 (87:91:97:101) sts], then dec 1 st

at each end of the next row and 4 (4:5:6:7) foll alt rows. [73 (77:79:83:85) sts.]
Work straight until armhole measures 7½ (7½:8:8¼:8½) in (19 (19:20:21:22) cm) from beg of shaping, ending with a WS row.

Shape shoulders

Bind off 4 (5:5:5:5) sts at beg of the next 2 rows, 5 (5:5:5:6) sts on the foll 2 rows, 5 (5:5:6:6) on the foll 2 rows, 5 (5:6:6:6) on the foll 2 rows. Leave rem 35 (37:37:39:39) sts on a st holder for back neck.

FRONT

Work as given for Back until Front measures 18 rows shorter than Back to beg of shoulder shaping, ending with a WS row.

Shape front neck

Knit 30 (31:32:33:34) sts, turn and leave rem sts on a st holder. Work on these sts for first side.
Dec 1 st at neck edge on the next 9 rows, then on the 2 foll alt rows. [19 (20:21:22:23) sts.]
Work 4 rows, ending with a WS row.

Shape shoulder

Bind off 4 (5:5:5:5) sts at beg of the next row, 5 (5:5:5:6) sts on the foll alt row, 5 (5:5:6:6) sts on the foll alt row, work 1 row then bind off rem 5 (5:6:6:6) sts.
With RS facing, slip the center

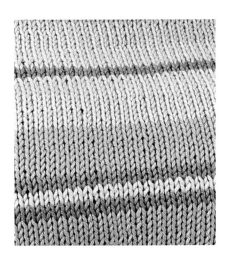

13 (15:15:17:17) sts on a st holder, rejoin yarn, and knit to end. Complete this side to match first side, reversing shapings.

SLEEVES (MAKE 2)

With US 2/3 (3 mm) needles and A, cast on 44 (48:48:50:50) sts and knit 9 rows. Change to US 5 (3¾ mm) needles. Work 130 rows to armhole, in stripe sequence and sleeve shaping as follows:

6 rows in B, 4 rows in C, 2 rows in D, 4 rows in C, 6 rows in B, 8 rows in A, 2 rows in D, 2 rows in C, 2 rows in D, (work the 44 rows of stripe patt) twice, then cont in stripe patt work 6 rows in A, at the same time shape sleeve by inc 1 st at each end of the 5th row, then every 6th row 2 (6:14:14:18) times, every 8th row 12 (9:3:3:0) times.
[74 (80:84:86:88) sts.]
Cont straight until all 130 rows are completed.

Shape sleeve top

Bind off 6 (7:8:8:9) sts at beg of the next 2 rows [62 (66:68:70:70) sts], then dec 1 st at each end of the next and 11 (10:13:13:17) foll alt rows [38 (44:40:42:34) sts], then at each end of the next 11 (13:11:11:7) rows. Bind off rem 16 (18:18:20:20) sts.

NECKBAND

Join left shoulder. With RS facing, US 2/3 (3 mm) needles and A, knit across 35 (37:37: 39:39) sts from back neck st holder, knit up 22 sts down left front neck, knit across 13 (15:15:17:17) sts from front neck st holder, knit up 22 sts up right front neck. [92 (96:96: 100:100) sts.]
Knit 9 rows. Bind off.

TO FINISH

Join right shoulder and neckband.
Sew sleeve tops into armholes, then join side and sleeve seams.

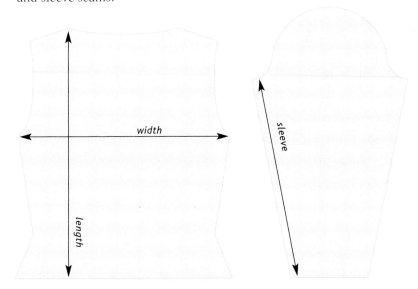

This extra-long cardigan is worked in the seed stitch and its striped design is a lovely counterpoint to its hand knitted loop stitch collar and ribbon tie. The cardigan is great for wearing with a simple pair of pants.

CARDIGAN WITH LOOP STITCH COLLAR

 ★★☆ MEDIUM

 This cardigan is very easy to knit, but the loop stitch collar takes a little more time to complete.

MEASUREMENTS
To fit bust

32	34	36	38	40	42	in
81	86	91	97	102	107	cm

Actual width

35	37	39	41	43	45	in
89	94	99	104	109	114	cm

Actual length

22¾	23¾	24	24½	25¼	26	in
58	60	61	62	64	66	cm

Actual sleeve seam

17	18	18	18	18	18½	in
43	46	46	46	46	47	cm

In the instructions, figures are given for the smallest size first; larger sizes follow in parentheses. Where only one set of figures is given, this applies to all sizes.

MATERIALS
- 8 (8:9:9:10:10) × 50 g balls of Rowan Summer Tweed in Storm 521 (A)
- 4 (4:4:5:5:5) × 50 g balls of Rowan Summer Tweed in Summer Berry 537 (B)
- 2 × 100 g balls of Rowan Yorkshire Tweed in Darkside 414 (C)
- Pair each of US 6 (4 mm) and US 8 (5 mm) needles
- 7 buttons
- Ribbon for front tie

GAUGE
16 sts and 28 rows to 4 in (10 cm) measured over seed stitch using US 8 (5 mm) needles.

ABBREVIATIONS
See page 10.

CARDIGAN

BACK
With US 8 (5 mm) needles and A, cast on 71 (75:79:83:87:91) sts. Purl 2 rows.
Cont in seed st patt and stripe patt and shaping for sides as follows:
Rows 1 to 12: With A, *k1, p1; rep from * to last st, k1. (This row forms the seed st patt and is repeated throughout)
Row 13: As row 1, dec 1 st at each end of row. [69 (73:77:81:85:89) sts.]
Row 14: As row 1.
Rows 15 to 18: With C, work in seed st.
Row 19: With B, work as row 1, dec 1 st at each end of row. [67 (71:75:79:83:87) sts.]
Row 20: With B, work in seed st.
These 20 rows form the stripe patt (14 rows in A, 4 rows in C, 2 rows in B).
Cont in stripe patt throughout.
Work 4 rows in A, then cont to shape sides by dec 1 st at each end of the next and foll 6th rows twice [61 (65:69:73:77:81) sts], then inc 1 st at each end of the foll 14th row, then every 10th row 4 times. [71 (75:79:83:87:91) sts.]

Cont straight in patt until work measures 15½ (16:16:16:16½:17) in (39 (41:41:41:42:43) cm), ending with a WS row.

Shape armholes

Bind off 4 (4:5:5:6:6) sts at beg of the next 2 rows [63 (67:69:73:75:79) sts], then dec 1 st at each end of the next and 4 (4:4:5:5:6) foll alt rows. [53 (57:59:61:63:65) sts.] Cont straight in patt until armhole measures 7½ (7½:8:8¼:8¾:9) in (19 (19:20:21:22:23) cm), ending with a WS row.

Shape shoulders and back neck

Bind off 5 (5:6:6:6:6) sts at beg of the next row, patt to 13 (15:15:15:16:17) sts on RH needle after bind-off, turn, and leave rem sts on a st holder. Work on these sts for first side. Work 3 rows, dec 1 st at neck edge on every row and binding off 5 (6:6:6:6:7) sts for shoulder on 2nd row. Bind off rem 5 (6:6:6:7:7) sts. With RS facing, rejoin yarn to rem sts and bind off center 17 (17:17:19:19:19) sts, then patt to end. Complete this side to match first side, reversing shapings.

LEFT FRONT

With US 8 (5 mm) needles and A, cast on 35 (37:39:41:43:45) sts and purl 2 rows.
Cont in seed st and stripe patt as Back. Work

12 rows, then shape sides by dec 1 st at RH edge on the next, then every 6th row 4 times [30 (32:34:36:38:40) sts], then inc 1 st at same edge on the foll 14th row, then every 10th row 4 times. [35 (37:39:41:43:45) sts.] Work straight until Front matches Back to beg of armhole shaping, ending with the same patt row and at side edge.

Shape armhole and front edge

Bind off 4 (4:5:5:6:6) sts at beg of the next row. [31 (33:34:36:37:39) sts.] Work 1 row. Dec 1 st at each end of the next row. [29 (31:32:34:35:37) sts.] Work 8 (8:8:10:10:12) rows dec 1 st at armhole edge on the 4 (4:4:5:5:6) foll alt rows, and dec 1 st at front edge every 4th row 2 (2:2:2:2:3) times. [23 (25:26:27:28:28) sts.] Keeping armhole edge straight, work 24 (24:24:28:28:12) rows dec 1 st at front edge as set on every 4th row, then work 12 (12:12:12:12:30) rows dec 1 st on every 6th row. [15 (17:18:18:19:20) sts.] Cont straight in patt until Front measures the same as the Back to beg of shoulder shaping, ending at armhole edge.

Shape shoulder

Bind off 5 (5:6:6:6:6) sts at beg of the next row, 5 (6:6:6:6:7) sts on the foll alt row. Work 1 row. Bind off rem 5 (6:6:6:7:7) sts.

RIGHT FRONT

Work as given for Left Front, reversing shapings.

SLEEVES (MAKE 2)

With US 8 (5 mm) needles and A, cast on
39 (39:41:41:43:43) sts. Purl 2 rows.
Cont in seed st and stripe patt as Back beg
with a 9th (7th:7th:7th:9th:11th) patt row.
Inc 1 st at each end of the 11th
(13th:9th:9th:9th:7th) row, then every
12th (14th:10th:10th:10th:8th) row
3 (7:3:3:10:1) times [47 (55:49:49:65:47) sts],
then every 14th (10th:12th:12th:0th:10th)
row 4 (0:6:6:0:10) times. [55 (55:61:61:65:67)
sts.] Cont straight in patt until Sleeve
measures 17 (18:18:18:18:18½) in
(43 (46:46:46:46:47) cm) from beg, ending
with the same patt row as Back to beg of
armhole shaping.

Shape sleeve top

Bind off 4 (4:5:5:6:6) sts at beg of the next
2 rows. [47 (47:51:51:53:55) sts.] Dec 1 st at
each end of the next and 3 (3:4:4:3:3) foll alt
rows, then every 4th row 4 (4:4:4:6:6) times,
then on the next 9 rows.
[13 (13:15:15:15:17) sts.] Bind off.

BUTTON BAND

With US 6 (4 mm) needles and A, cast on 7 sts.
Row 1: RS. K2, (p1, k1) twice, k1.
Row 2: (K1, p1) 3 times, k1.

Rep these 2 rows until button band is long
enough to fit along left front edge to beg of
front edge shaping. Bind off in rib.
Sew to front edge, then mark the positions of
7 buttons, the first to come 4 rows up from
cast-on edge, the last 4 rows down from bind-
off edge, and the remainder spaced evenly
between.

BUTTONHOLE BAND

Work as given for Button band making
buttonholes to correspond with markers as
follows:
Buttonhole row 1: RS. Rib 3, bind off 1 st,
rib to end.
Buttonhole row 2: In rib, casting on over
bound-off st on previous row.

COLLAR

Join shoulders.

Left side

With US 8 (5 mm) needles and B, cast on
5 sts.
Row 1: WS. Knit.
Row 2: K3, inc (by knitting and purling into
next st), k1, 6 sts.
Row 3: K1, inc in next st, k to end. [7 sts.]
Row 4: *K1 keeping st on LH needle bring yf,
pass yarn over left thumb to make a loop
approximately 1½ in (4 cm), yb and knit this st
again, slipping st off the needle, yfon pass the

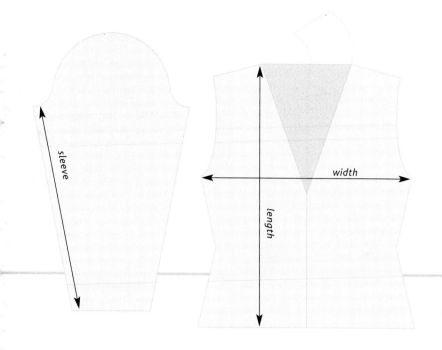

JACKET

BACK

With US 10½ (6½ mm) needles cast on 57 (61:65:69:71) sts. Cont in seed st as follows:
Row 1: *K1, p1; rep from * to last st, k1.
Rep this row throughout.
Shape sides by dec 1 st at each end of the 7th, then every 8th row 4 times [47 (51:55:59:61) sts], then inc 1 st at each end of the foll 8th row, then every 6th row 4 times.
[57 (61:65:69:71) sts.] Work straight until work measures 15½ (16:16:16:16½) in (39 (41:41:41:42) cm) from beg.

Shape armholes

Bind off 3 (3:4:5:5) sts at beg of the next 2 rows [51 (55:57:59:61) sts], then dec 1 st at each end of the 4 foll alt rows.
[43 (47:49:51:53) sts.] Cont straight until armhole measures 7½ (7½:8:8¼:8¼) in (19 (19:20:21:22) cm) from beg of shaping.

Shape shoulders and back neck

Bind off 4 (4:5:4:5) sts at beg of the next row, patt until there are 11 (13:13:13:13) sts on RH needle, turn, and work on these sts for first side. Work 3 rows dec 1 st at neck edge on every row and binding off 4 (5:5:5:5) sts for shoulder on 2nd row. Bind off rem 4 (5:5:5:5) sts. Rejoin yarn and bind off center 13 (13:13:17:17) sts, patt to end. Complete this side to match first side, reversing shapings.

LEFT FRONT

With US 10½ (6½ mm) needles, cast on 33 (35:37:39:41) sts. Cont in seed st as Back, shaping sides by dec 1 st at RH edge on the 7th, then every 8th row 4 times [28 (30:32:34:36) sts], then inc 1 st at same edge on the foll 8th row, then every 6th row 4 times. [33 (35:37:39:41) sts.] Work straight until Front measures the same as the Back to beg of armhole shaping, ending at side edge.

Shape armhole

Bind off 3 (3:4:5:5) sts at beg of the next row [30 (32:33:34:36) sts], dec 1 st at the same edge on the 4 foll alt rows.
[26 (28:29:30:32) sts.] Cont straight until Front measures 13 rows shorter than Back to beg of shoulder shaping, ending at front edge.

COLLAR NOTCH

Bind off 5 sts in seed st patt, turn, and cast on 5 sts, patt to end.
Cont in patt until Front measures the same as the Back to beg of shoulder shaping, ending at side edge.

FRINGING FOR JACKET

For each tassel, cut 2 lengths of yarn, each 2¾ in (7 cm) long, fold in half then tie in approximately ¾ in (1.5 cm) in from edge, spacing ¼ in (1 cm) apart (see page 13). Repeat all around collar edge, around outer edge on pockets (not top pocket), and cuffs. Trim ends to neaten.

Shape shoulder

Bind off 4 (4:5:4:5) sts at beg of the next row, 4 (5:5:5:5) sts on the 2 foll alt rows. Cont on the rem 14 (14:14:16:17) sts for collar to center of back neck. Bind off in patt. Mark the positions of 2 buttons, the first 5½ in (14 cm) and the second 9½ in (24 cm) up from cast-on edge.

RIGHT FRONT

Work as given for Left Front, reversing shapings and working buttonholes at RH edge to correspond with markers.

Buttonhole row 1: Patt 3, (yo) twice, k2tog, patt to end.

Buttonhole row 2: In patt dropping one yo from previous row.

POCKETS (MAKE 2)

With US 10½ (6½ mm) needles cast on 11 sts. Cont in seed st. Work 1 row, then inc 1 st at each end of the next 3 rows. [17 sts.] Cont straight until pocket measures 4¾ in (12 cm) from beg. Cast off in patt.

SLEEVES (MAKE 2)

With US 10½ (6½ mm) needles cast on 31 (31:33:33:35) sts and cont in seed st as Back, at the same time inc 1 st at each end of the 9th (11th:11th:11th:7th) row, then every 10th (11th:11th:11th:8th) row 1 (7:7:7:1) time(s) [35 (47:49:49:39) sts] then every 12th (0:0:0:10th) row 5 (0:0:0:7) times.

[45 (47:49:49:53) sts.] Cont straight until sleeve measures 17 (18:18:18:18) in (43 (46:46:46:46) cm) from beg.

Shape sleeve top

Bind off 3 (3:4:5:5) sts at beg of the next 2 rows [39 (41:41:39:43) sts], then dec 1 st at each end of the 5 (5:6:6:7) foll alt rows [29 (31:29:27:29) sts], then every 4th row 2 times [25 (27:25:23:25) sts], then on the next 7 rows. Cast off rem 11 (13:11:9:11) sts in patt.

TO FINISH

Join shoulders. Join collar seam, then sew to back of neck. Sew sleeve tops into armholes, then join side and sleeve seams.

Sew pockets centrally on fronts, positioning bottom of pocket 2 in (5 cm) up from cast-on edge. Sew on buttons. Add fringing (see left).

SLEEVELESS TOP

BACK AND FRONT (ALIKE)

With US 3 (3¼ mm) needles and A, cast on 81 (89:97:101:105) sts. Work seed st border.

Row 1: *K1, p1; rep from * to last st, k1. Rep this row 5 times more.

Change to US 6 (4 mm) needles and cont in patt as follows:

Preparation rows:

Row 1: WS. With A, purl.

Row 2: With A, knit.

Row 3: With A, p2, *p1 wrapping yarn twice, p3; rep from * end last rep p2.

End of preparation rows.

Row 4: With B, k2, *sl 1 wyib dropping extra wrap, k1, insert needle into next st 2 rows below and draw through a loop loosely, knit next st, and pass the loop over the st just knitted, k1; rep from * end sl 1 wyib, k2.

Row 5: With B, p2, *sl 1 wyif, p3; rep from * end sl 1 wyif, p2.

Row 6: With B, knit.

Row 7: With B, p2, *p1, wrapping yarn twice, p3; rep from * end last rep p2.

Rows 8 to 11: With A rep Rows 4 to 7.

Rep Rows 4 to 11 throughout.

Cont in patt until work measures 13½ in (34 cm) from beg, ending with a WS row.

Shape armholes

Bind off 6 (6:7:7:7) sts at beg of the next 2 rows [69 (77:83:87:91) sts], then dec 1 st at each end of the next 4 rows [61 (69:75:79:83) sts], then at each end of the 3 foll alt rows. [55 (63:69:73:77) sts.]

Cont straight until armhole measures 5½ (6 6¼:6¾:7) in (14 (15:16:17:18) cm) from beg of shaping, ending with a WS row.

Shape neck

Patt 13, turn, and leave rem sts on a st holder. Work on these sts for first side. Patt 1 row.

Work 11 rows dec 1 st at neck edge on every row. [2 sts.] Bind off.

With RS facing, slip the center 29 (37:43:47:51) sts on a st holder, rejoin yarn to rem 13 sts, and patt to end. Complete this side to match first side, reversing shapings.

NECKBAND

Join left shoulder. With RS facing, US 3 (3¼ mm) needles and A, knit up 12 sts along right back neck edge, knit across 29 (37:43:47:51) sts from back neck st holder, knit up 12 sts along left back neck, 12 sts along left front neck, knit across 29 (37:43:47:51) sts from front neck st holder, knit up 13 sts up right front neck. [107 (123:135:143:151) sts.]

Work 5 rows in seed st as for lower edge. Bind off in seed st.

ARMBANDS (MAKE 2)

Join right shoulder and neckband. With RS facing, US 3 (3¼ mm) needles and A, knit up 91 (97:103:107:113) sts evenly along armhole edge. Work 5 rows in seed st as for lower edge. Bind off in seed st.

TO FINISH

Join sides and armhole borders. Add fringing (see above right).

FRINGING FOR TOP

For each tassel, cut 2 lengths of yarn A, each 2¾ in (7 cm) long, fold in half, and tie in along first row worked for neckband approximately ½ in (1 cm) apart (see page 13). Repeat all around neckband. Trim edges to neaten.

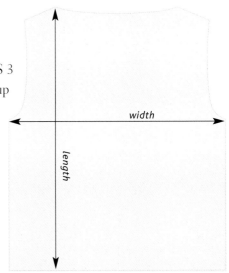

Work 38 (40:46) rows dec 1 st at each end of the next and every foll alt row.
Bind off rem 21 (23:23) sts.

LEFT FRONT

Working from outside of the ball, with US 5 (3¾ mm) needles, cast on 39 (45:51) sts.
Work 2½ in (6 cm) in rib as given for Back, ending with a RS row.
Next row: Rib 9, leave these 9 sts on a st holder for Left Front border, rib to end inc 2 sts evenly across row for 1st size only and dec 3 sts evenly across row for 3rd size only. [32 (36:39) sts.]
Change to US 7 (4½ mm) needles and cont in st st. Work 10 (10:14) rows.
Work 19 rows dec 1 st at beg of the next and every foll 6th row. [28 (32:35) sts.]
Work 11 rows without shaping.
Work 25 rows inc 1 st at beg of the next and

every foll 8th row. [32 (36:39) sts.]
Work straight until left front measures 15 (15:15¾) in (38 (38:40) cm) from beg, ending with a WS row.

Shape raglan

Next row: Bind off 4 sts, knit to end. [28 (32:35) sts.]
Next row: Purl.
Work 2 (4:4) rows dec 1 st at raglan edge on every row. [26 (28:31) sts.]
Work 29 (31:33) rows dec 1 st at raglan edge on the next and every foll alt row. [11 (12:14) sts.]

Shape neck

Next row: Bind off 3 (4:4) sts, purl to end. [8 (8:10) sts.]
Work 2 rows dec 1 st at raglan edge on the next row, at the same time dec 1 st at neck edge on every row. [5 (5:7) sts.]
Work 5 (5:9) rows dec 1 st at raglan edge only on next and every foll alt row. [2 sts.]
Next row: P2tog. Fasten off.

RIGHT FRONT

Working from outside of the ball, with US 5 (3¾ mm) needles, cast on 39 (45:51) sts.
Work 2 rows in rib as given for Back.
Row 3: Rib 4, bind off 2 sts, rib to end.
Row 4: Rib to 4 sts, cast on 2 sts, rib 4.
Cont in rib for 2½ in (6 cm), ending with a RS row.

Next row: Rib to last 9 sts, inc 2 sts evenly across row for 1st size only and dec 3 sts across row for 3rd size only, slip rem 9 sts onto a st holder for Right Front border. [32 (36:39) sts.] Change to US 7 (4½ mm) needles and cont in st st. Work 10 (10:14) rows. Work 19 rows dec 1 st end of the next and every foll 6th row. [28 (32:35) sts.] Work 11 rows without shaping. Work 25 rows inc 1 st at end of the next and every foll 8th row. [32 (36:39) sts.] Work straight until right front measures 15 (15:15¾) in(38 (38:40) cm) from beg, ending with a RS row.

Shape raglan

Next row: Bind off 4 sts, purl to end. [28 (32:35) sts.]
Work 2 (4:4) rows dec 1 st at raglan edge on every row. [26 (28:31) sts.]
Work 28 (30:32) rows dec 1 st at raglan edge on the next and every foll alt row. [12 (13:15) sts.]

Shape neck

Next row: Bind off 3 (4:4) sts, knit to last 2 sts, k2tog. [8 (8:10) sts.]
Next row: Purl.
Work 2 rows dec 1 st at neck edge on every row, at the same time dec 1 st at raglan edge on the next row. [5 (5:7) sts.]
Work 5 (5:9) rows dec 1 st at raglan edge only on the next and every foll alt row. [2 sts.]
Next row: P2tog. Fasten off.

LEFT SLEEVE

Working from the center of the ball, with US 5 (3¾ mm) needles, cast on 33 sts. Work in rib as given for Back for 2½ in (6 cm), ending with a WS row.
Change to US 7 (4½ mm) needles and cont in rib as for Back throughout, inc 1 st at each end of the 5th and every foll 8th (6th:2nd) row to 55 (43:39) sts, working inc sts in rib.

2nd and 3rd sizes only

Inc 1 st at each end of every foll (8th:6th) row to (57:63) sts, working inc sts in rib.

All sizes

Work straight until sleeve measures 18 (18:18½) in (46 (46:47) cm) from beg, ending with a WS row.

Shape raglans

Bind off 4 sts at beg of the next 2 rows. [47 (49:55) sts.]
Work 12 (16:16) rows dec 1 st at each end of the next and every foll 4th row. [41 (41:47) sts.]
Work 28 (28:34) rows dec 1 st at each end of the next and every foll alt row.
Bind off rem 13 sts.

RIGHT SLEEVE

Working from outside of the ball, work as given for Left Sleeve.

HELPFUL HINT

Always knit to the recommended gauge. Knit up a gauge swatch before you start (see page 9) and make the necessary adjustments to achieve the correct gauge. If you knit too loosely, the stitches will rub against each other and cause pilling; if you knit too tightly, the garment will be stiff and less comfortable to wear.

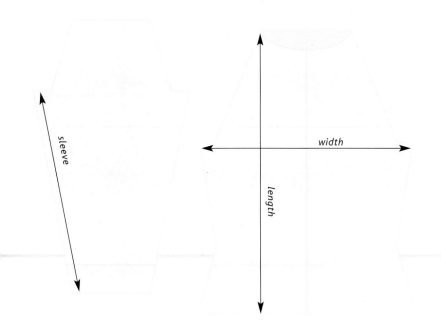

sleeve

width

length

LEFT FRONT BAND

With RS facing and US 5 (3¾ mm) needles,
cast on 1 st (cast on st used to sew band to
front), rib across 9 sts left on a st holder.
[10 sts.]

Row 1: P3, k3, p3, k1.

Row 2: P1, k3, p3, k3.

Rep these 2 rows until band is long enough to
fit up front to beg of neck shaping, ending
with a WS row. Break yarn and leave these sts
on a st holder.

Mark the position of 6 buttons, the first to
come 3 rows up from cast-on edge, the last
4 rows down from top and the remainder
spaced evenly between.

RIGHT FRONT BAND

With WS facing and US 5 (3¾ mm) needles,
cast on 1 st (cast-on st used to sew band to
front), rib across 9 sts left on st holder. [10 sts.]

Row 1: K3, p3, k3, p1.

Row 2: K1, p3, k3, p3.

Rep these 2 rows, working buttonhole rows as
given for Right Front to correspond with
markers on Left Front Border until band is
long enough to fit up front to beg of neck
shaping, ending with a WS row. Do not break
off yarn.

NECKBAND

Join raglan seams.

With RS facing and US 5 (3¾ mm) needles rib
across 10 sts at top of Right Front Band as
follows: k3, p3, k2, k2tog, knit up 11 (13:16) sts
evenly along right side of neck, 13 sts evenly
across top of left sleeve, 21 (23:23) sts evenly
across back of neck, 13 sts evenly across top of
right sleeve, 11 (13:16) sts evenly along left side
of neck and work across 10 sts left on st holder
at top of Left Front Band as follows: k2tog, k2,
p3, k3.

[87 (93:99) sts.]

Next row: Rib 9, p9 (9:10), inc in next st,
(p9 (10:11), inc in next st) 5 times,
p9 (10:10), rib 9. [93 (99:105) sts.]

Beg with a 1st row, work 18 rows in rib as
given for Back.

Next row: Rib 4, bind off 2 sts, rib to end.

Next row: Rib to last 4 sts, cast on 2 sts, rib 4.

Work 3 rows in rib.

Bind off loosely in rib.

TO FINISH

Join side and sleeve seams. Sew front bands in
position (using cast-on sts). Sew on buttons.

This easy-to-wear cape is knitted in two different colors and types of yarn, which complement each other. Garter stitch ridges add extra texture.

TWO-COLOR CAPE

MEASUREMENTS

To fit bust

32–36	38–42	in
81–91	97–107	cm

Actual length (excluding fringing)

22¾	23¾	in
58	60	cm

Actual width round lower edge

71	78	in
180	198	cm

In the instructions, figures are given for the smallest size first; larger size follows in parentheses. Where only one set of figures is given, this applies to both sizes.

MATERIALS

- 3 (4) × 100 g balls of Rowan Plaid in Red 156 (A)
- 4 (5) × 100 g balls of Rowan Chunky Print in Black 079 (B)
- Pair each of US 10 (6 mm) and US 11 (8 mm) needles
- Stitch holders
- 2 buttons (1 large, 1 small)

GAUGE

11½ sts and 15½ rows to 4 in (10 cm) measured over stockinette stitch using US 11 (8 mm) needles.

ABBREVIATIONS

See page 10.

CAPE

RIGHT SIDE (BACK AND FRONT WORKED IN ONE PIECE)

With US 10 (6 mm) needles and A, cast on 104 (114) sts. Knit 4 rows.
Change to US 11 (8 mm) needles. Cont in patt as follows:
Work 8 rows in st st, beg with a knit row.
Row 13 (dec row): K25 (28), sl 1, k1, psso, k50 (54), k2tog, k25 (28). [102 (112) sts.]
St st 5 more rows. Knit 4 rows.
Row 23 (dec row): K25 (28), sl 1, k1, psso, k48 (52), k2tog, k25 (28). [100 (110) sts.]
Knit 1 row.
Work 8 rows in st st.
Row 33 (dec row): K25 (28), sl 1, k1, psso, k46 (50), k2tog, k25 (28). [98 (108) sts.]
St st 5 more rows.
Cont in this way, working patt – 6 rows in g st and 14 rows in st st throughout, at the same time dec in the same way as before on the next and foll 6th row. [94 (104) sts.]
Then dec every 4th row 3 times, then on the 18 (20) foll alt rows. [52 (58) sts.]
Work 1 row.
Next row: K25 (28), sl 1, k1, psso, k25 (28). [51 (57) sts.]
Next row: Purl.

This is a really straightforward and simple pattern, which can be knitted up in a short amount of time.

length

Next row: K4, *k2tog, k5(2); rep from
* 6 (12) times, k2tog, k3. [44 sts.]
Next row: Purl and leave sts on a st holder.

LEFT SIDE (BACK AND FRONT WORKED IN ONE PIECE)

With US 10 (6 mm) needles and B, cast on
104 (114) sts. Knit 4 rows.
Change to US 11 (8 mm) needles and cont as
given for Right Side.

TO FINISH

Join center back seam.

NECKBAND

With RS facing and using US 10 (6 mm)
needles and B, knit across 43 sts from right
side, k2tog, knit rem 43 sts from left side.
[87 sts.]
Knit 1 row. Bind off.

FRONT EDGES (MAKE 2)

With RS facing and using Us 10 (6 mm)
needles and B, knit up 78 sts along one front
edge. Knit 1 row. Bind off.

Sew the large button 4¾ in (12 cm) in from
left front edge and the small button at the
same distance on the wrong side on right
front. Sew a loop on each top edge to
correspond with buttons.
For each tassel, cut 4 strands of yarn
approximately 9¾ in (25 cm) long and tie in
fringing evenly along lower edge (see Making
Tassels, page 13). Work fringing in A on front
worked in B, and in B on front worked in A.

This travel-easy, ribbed and cabled cardigan with hood has cross stitch details that have been worked in a complementary color along the sleeves and body, adding a touch of elegance.

HOODED CARDIGAN WITH EMBROIDERY

★★☆ MEDIUM

 *Some knitting skill is needed to create the cable pattern and cross stitch embroidery.*

Inserting the zip requires neat finishing.

MEASUREMENTS
To fit bust

32–34	36–38	40–42	in
81–86	91–97	102–107	cm

Actual width

36½	41¼	44¼	in
92.5	105	112.5	cm

Actual length (from shoulder)
28 in (71 cm)

Actual sleeve seam

17¼	18	18½	in
44	46	47	cm

In the instructions, figures are given for the smallest size first; larger sizes follow in parentheses. Where only one set of figures is given this applies to all sizes.

MATERIALS
- 11 (12:13) × 50 g balls of Rowan Cork 047
- 1 × 50 g ball of Rowan Handknit DK Cotton for embroidery in 313
- Pair each of US 10½ (6½ mm) and US 11 (8 mm) needles
- Cable needle
- Stitch holders
- 28 in (71 cm) open ended zipper

GAUGE
16 sts and 19 rows to 4 in (10 cm) measured over pattern using US 11 (8 mm) needles.

ABBREVIATIONS
C6 – slip 3 sts onto a cable needle and hold at front, k3 then k3 from cable needle.
See also page 10.

CARDIGAN

BACK
With US 10½ (6½ mm) needles cast on 74 (84:90) sts.

1st and 3rd sizes
Row 1: RS. K1, p1, *k6, p2; rep from * to last 8 sts, k6, p1, k1.
Row 2: K2, *p6, k2; rep from * to end.

2nd size
Row 1: RS. K5, *p2, k6; rep from * to last 7 sts, p2, k5.
Row 2: K1, p4, *k2, p6; rep from * to last 7 sts, k2, p4, k1.

All sizes
Work a further 10 rows as now set.
Change to US 11 (8 mm) needles. Cont in patt as follows:

1st size
Row 13: K1, p1, *C6, p2, k6, p2; rep from * to last 8 sts, C6, p1, k1.
Row 14: K2, *p6, k2; rep from * to end.

2nd size
Row 13: K5, *p2, C6, p2, k6; rep from * to last 15 sts, p2, C6, p2, k5.
Row 14: K1, p4, *k2, p6; rep from * to last 7 sts, k2, p4, k1.

CROSS STITCH

This can be worked singly (as here) or in blocks. Work a row of diagonal stitches from left to right and complete the crosses by working diagonal stitches back from right to left. Choose a nice contrast color.

3rd size

Row 13: K1, p1, *k6, p2, C6, p2; rep from * to last 8 sts, k6, p1, k1.

Row 14: K2, *p6, k2; rep from * to end.

All sizes

Rows 15, 17, 19, 21 and 23: As row 1.

Rows 16, 18, 20, 22 and 24: As row 2.

Rep rows 13 to 24 throughout. Cont in patt until work measures 19 (18:17¼) in (48 (46:44) cm) from beg, ending with a WS row.

Shape raglans

Bind off 5 (6:7) sts at beg of the next 2 rows. [64 (72:76) sts.]

Next row: K2, k2tog, patt to the last 4 sts, k2tog-tbl, k2.

Next row: K1, p2, patt to last 3 sts, p2, k1. Rep the last 2 rows 20 (22:24) times more, leave rem 22 (26:26) sts on a st holder.

LEFT FRONT

With US 10½ (6½ mm) needles cast on 40 (45:48) sts.

1st and 3rd sizes

Row 1: RS. K1, p1, *k6, p2; rep from * to last 6 sts, (k1, p1) twice, k2.

Row 2: (K1, p1) 3 times, k2, *p6, k2; rep from * to end.

2nd size

Row 1: RS. K5, p2; *k6, p2; rep from * to last 6 sts, (k1, p1) twice, k2.

Row 2: (K1, p1) 3 times, k2, *p6, k2; rep from * to last 5 sts, p4, k1.

All sizes

Work a further 10 rows as now set. **
Change to US 12 (8 mm) needles. Cont in patt as follows:

1st size

Row 13: K1, p1, *C6, p2, k6, p2; rep from * to last 6 sts, (k1, p1) twice, k2.

Row 14: (K1, p1) 3 times, k2, *p6, k2; rep from * to end.

2nd size

Row 13: K5, p2, *C6, p2, k6, p2; rep from * to last 6 sts, (k1, p1) twice, k2.

Row 14: (K1, p1) 3 times, k2, *p6, k2; rep from * to last 5 sts, p4, k1.

3rd size

Row 13: K1, p1, *k6, p2, C6, p2; rep from * to last 14 sts, k6, p2, (k1, p1) twice, k2.

Row 14: (K1, p1) 3 times, k2, *p6, k2; rep from * to end.

All sizes

Rows 15 to 24: As Back.

Cont in patt as given for Back until work measures same as Back to beg of raglan shaping, ending with a WS row (RS on right front).

Shape raglan

Bind off 5 (6:7) sts at beg of the next row. [35 (39:41) sts]. Work 1 row. (Omit this row on Right Front.)

Next row: K2, k2tog, patt to end.
Next row: Patt to last 3 sts, p2, k1.
Rep these 2 rows, 20 (22:24) times more.
[14 (16:16) sts.] Leave sts on a st holder.

RIGHT FRONT
Work as given for Left Front to **.
Change to US 11 (8 mm) needles. Cont in patt as follows:

1st size
Row 13: K2, (p1, k1) twice, *p2, k6, p2, C6; rep from * to last 2 sts, p1, k1.

2nd size
Row 13: K2, (p1, k1) twice, p2, *k6, p2, C6, p2; rep from * to last 5 sts, k5.

3rd size
Row 13: K2, (p1, k1) twice, p2; *k6, p2, C6, p2; rep from * to last 8 sts, k6, p1, k1.
Cont as now set. Complete as given for Left Front, reversing shapings, ending with a WS row. Leave sts on a st holder.

SLEEVES (MAKE 2)
With US 10½ (6½ mm) needles cast on 34 (38:42) sts.
Row 1: RS. P0 (0:2), k4 (6:6), *p2, k6; rep from * to last 6 (8:10) sts, p2, k4 (6:6), p0 (0:2).
Row 2: K0 (0, 2), p4 (6:6), k2, *p6, k2; rep from * to last 4 (6:8) sts, p4 (6:6), k0 (0:2).
Work a further 10 rows as now set.
Change to US 11 (8 mm) needles. **

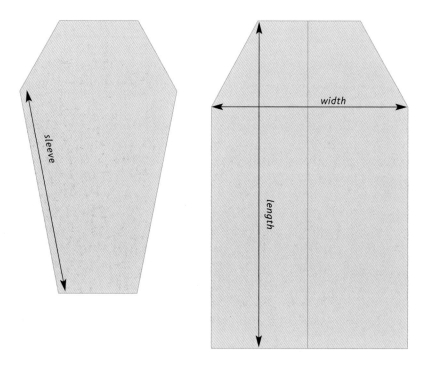

sleeve

width

length

Row 13: P0 (0:2), k4 (6:6), p2, C6, p2, k6, p2, C6, p2, k4 (6:6), p0 (0:2).
Rep rows 13 to 24 as given for Back, at the same time inc 1 st at each end every 4 rows 1 (1:2) time(s) [36 (40:46) sts], then every 6th row 9 (10:10) times [54 (60:66) sts], working patt into inc sts. Cont straight until sleeve measures 17¼ (18:18½) in (44 (46:47) cm) from beg, ending with a WS row.

Shape raglans

Bind off 5 (6:7) sts at beg of the next 2 rows. [44 (48:52) sts.]
Row 1: K2, k2tog, patt to last 4 sts, k2tog-tbl, k2.

Rows 2 and 4: K1, p2, patt to last 3 sts, p2, k1.
Row 3: K3, patt to last 3 sts, k3.
Rep the last 4 rows, 4 times more [34 (38:42) sts], then dec 1 st at each end of the next and 10 (12:14) foll alt rows. [12 sts.]
Work 1 row. Leave sts on a st holder.

HOOD

Join raglans.
With RS facing and US 11 (8 mm) needles, rib 6, k8 (10:10) sts from right front st holder, knit across 12 sts from top of right sleeve, work across 22 (26:26) sts from back neck as follows: K6 (7:7), M1, (k5 (6:6), M1) twice, k6 (7:7), knit across 12 sts from top of left sleeve, then 8 (10:10) sts from left front, rib rem 6 sts as set. [77 (85:85) sts.]
Cont in st st beg with a purl row, keeping the 6 rib sts at each end on every row, until hood measures 13¾ in (35 cm) from beg, ending with a WS row. Bind off.

TO FINISH

Join hood seam. Join side and sleeve seams. Sew in zipper. Make a tassel using 6 strands of yarn approximately 10 in (25 cm) long (see Making Tassels, page 13). Fold in half, wind yarn ½ in (1.5 cm) down from folded end and secure, thread yarn through loop formed, and attach to point on back hood.
Work embroidered cross stitches on each rib between cables (see page 58).

Knitted with big yarn and big needles using stockinette stitch, this tweedy jacket with funky fur collar could be worn anywhere.

JACKET WITH FUNKY COLLAR

MEASUREMENTS

To fit bust

32–34	36–38	40–42	in
81–86	91–97	102–107	cm

Actual width

39½	43½	47¼	in
100	110	120	cm

Actual length

22½	23¼	24	in
57	59	61	cm

Actual sleeve seam
18 in (46 cm)

In the instructions, figures are given for the smallest size first; larger sizes follow in parentheses. Where only one set of figures is given, this applies to all sizes.

MATERIALS

- 9 (10:11) × 100 g balls of Sirdar Bigga in 674 (A)
- 2 (3:3) × 50 g balls of Sirdar New Fizz in 0802 (B)
- Pair each of US 17 (12¾ mm) and US 19 (15 mm) needles
- Stitch holder
- 7 buttons

GAUGE

6 sts and 9 rows to 4 in (10 cm) measured over stockinette stitch using US 19 (15 mm) needles.

ABBREVIATIONS

See page 10.

JACKET

BACK

With US 17 (12¾ mm) needles and A, cast on 29 (33:35) sts.

Row 1: RS. *K1, p1; rep from * to last st, k1.
Row 2: *P1, k1; rep from * to last st, p1.
These 2 rows form the rib. Work 2 more rows in rib inc 1 (0:1) st in center of last row. [30 (33:36) sts.]
Change to US 19 (15 mm) needles. Cont in st st, beg with a knit row.
Work 4 rows.
Dec row: K1, k2tog, knit to last 3 sts, sl 1, k1, psso, k1.
Work 3 rows then work the dec row once more. [26 (29:32) sts.]
Work 7 rows straight.
Inc row: K1, M1, knit to last st, M1, k1. [28 (31:34) sts.]
Rep the last 8 rows once more. [30 (33:36) sts.]
Cont straight as now set until work measures 13½ in (34 cm) from beg, ending with a WS row.

Shape armholes

Bind off 2 (3:4) sts at beg of the next 2 rows [26 (27:28) sts], then dec 1 st at both ends of

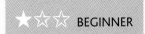 BEGINNER

This garment is easy to knit but requires some care when picking up the stitches on each front edge.

Work 7 rows.

Next row: Knit to last st, M1, k1.

Rep the last 8 rows once more.

[22 (24:26) sts.]

Cont until work measures the same as the Back to beg of armhole shaping, ending with a RS row.

Shape armhole

Bind off 2 (3:4) sts at beg of the next row.

[20 (21:22) sts.] Dec 1 st at armhole edge on the next and foll alt row.

[18 (19:20) sts.]

Cont straight until work measures 5 rows shorter than Back to left shoulder, ending at front edge.

Shape neck

Bind off 11 (12:13) sts at beg of the next row [7 sts], then dec 1 st at neck edge on the next 2 rows. [5 sts.]

Work 2 rows, ending at armhole edge.

Shape shoulder

Bind off 2 sts at beg of the next row. Work 1 row. Bind off rem 3 sts.

SLEEVES (MAKE 2)

With US 17 (12¾ mm) needles and A, cast on 13 (15:17) sts and work 4 rows in rib as given for Back inc 1 st in center on last row.

[14 (16:18) sts.]

Change to US 19 (15 mm) needles. Cont in st st, beg with a knit row. Work 4 rows, then inc 1 st at each end of the next, then every 6th row 4 times. [24 (26:28) sts.] Cont straight until sleeve measures 18 in (46 cm) from beg, ending with a WS row.

Shape sleeve top

Bind off 2 (3:4) sts at beg of the next 2 rows. [20 sts.]

Next row: K2tog, k to last 2 sts, sl 1, k1, psso. [18 sts.]

Dec 1 st at each end of every 4th row 0 (1:1) time(s). [18 (16:16) sts.] Dec 1 st at each end of the 3 (2:2) foll alt rows. [12 sts.]

Next row: WS. P2tog-tbl, purl to last 2 sts, p2tog. [10 sts.]

Work 3 more rows dec 1 st at each end of every row. [4 sts.] Bind off.

FRONT BANDS (MAKE 2)

With RS facing and using US 17 (12¾ mm) needles and A, knit up 35 (36:37) sts along one front edge. Knit 1 row. Bind off.

COLLAR

Note: The purl side is the right side of the work. Join shoulders.

With US 19 (15 mm) needles and B, cast on 106 (112:118) sts. Cont in st st until collar measures 8¼ in (21 cm) from beg.
Bind off loosely.

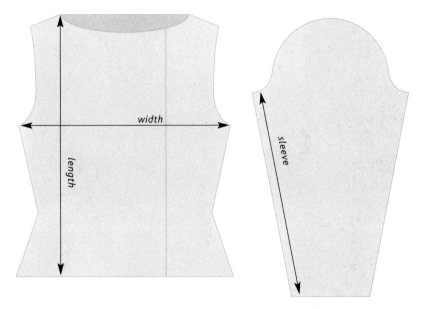

TO FINISH

Sew cast-on edge of collar to neck edge. Sew sleeve tops into armholes, then join side and sleeve seams. Sew on buttons. Use natural holes in fabric for buttons to fasten.

This glorious patchwork pattern is slightly more challenging to knit, but your efforts will be well worthwhile. The long coat with ribbed collar edged in tassels is worked primarily in stockinette stitch, and the finished results have an enduring appeal.

PATCHWORK COAT

★★★ ADVANCED

 The stitch used in this garment (stockinette stitch) is very simple to work.

 This project is slightly more challenging because of the number of color changes.

HELPFUL HINTS
- When working with different colored yarns, use the Intarsia technique. Twist the new color around the color just used to link the colors together and avoid holes. Do not break off and join in except where absolutely necessary.

MEASUREMENTS
To fit bust

32–36	38–42	in
81–91	97–107	cm

Actual width

45	50½	in
114	128	cm

Actual length

37	39	in
94	99	cm

Actual sleeve seam (with cuff turned back)

16	16½	in
41	42	cm

In the instructions, figures are given for the smallest size first; larger size follows in parentheses. Where only one set of figures is given, this applies to both sizes.

MATERIALS
- 4 (5) × 100 g balls of Sirdar Denim Chunky in Denim Blue Marl 516 (A)
- 3 (4) × 100 g balls of Sirdar Denim Chunky in Ivory Cream 508 (B)
- 2 (3) × 100 g balls of Sirdar Denim Chunky in Denim Blue 502 (C)
- 2 (3) × 100 g balls of Sirdar Denim Chunky in Camel 613 (D)
- Pair each of US 9 (5½ mm) and US 10½ (6½ mm) needles
- 4 toggles

TENSION
14 sts and 19 rows to 4 in (10 cm) measured over stockinette stitch using US 10½ (6½ mm) needles.

ABBREVIATIONS
See page 10.

COAT

BACK
With US 9 (5½ mm) needles and A, cast on 78 (90) sts.
Row 1: RS. *K2, p2; rep from * to last 2 sts, k2.
Row 2: *P2, k2; rep from * to last 2 sts, p2.
These 2 rows form the 2x2 rib. Work 8 more rows in rib inc 2 (0) sts evenly on last row. [80 (90) sts.]
Change to US 10½ (6½ mm) needles. Cont in patt as follows:
Row 1: RS. K8 (9) A, k16 (18) B, k16 (18) C, k16 (18) D, k16 (18) B, k8 (9) A.
Row 2: P8 (9) A, p16 (18) B, p16 (18) D, p16 (18) C, p16 (18) B, p8 (9) A.

Rep these 2 rows 16 (17) times more.
[34 (36) patt rows.]
Row 35 (37): K8 (9) C, k16 (18) D, k16 (18)
B, k16 (18) A, k16 (18) D, k8 (9) C.
Row 36 (38): P8 (9) C, p16 (18) D, p16 (18)
A, p16 (18) B, p16 (18) D, p8 (9) C.
Rep these 2 rows 16 (17) times more.
[34 (36) patt rows.]
Rep rows 1 to 68 (72), then rows 1 to 34 (36)
once more. Bind off.

LEFT FRONT

With US 9 (5½ mm) needles and A, cast on
38 (46) sts and work 10 rows in 2x2 rib as
given for Back inc 2 (dec 1) st evenly on last
row. [40 (45) sts.]
Change to US 10½ (6½ mm) needles. Cont in
patt as follows:
Row 1: RS. K8 (9) A, k16 (18) B, k16 (18) C.
Work a further 33 (35) rows as set.
Row 35 (37): K8 (9) C, k16 (18) D,
k16 (18) B.
Work a further 33 (35) rows as set.
Rep rows 1 to 34 (36), then rows 35 (37) to
52 (54) once, ending with a WS row.
[120 (126) rows.]

Shape front slope

Next row: Work in patt to the last 2 sts, sl 1,
k1, psso. Place a marker at end of row.
Patt 3 rows. Rep these 4 rows 6 (7) times
more, omitting markers. [33 (37) sts.]

Next row: Patt to the last 2 sts, sl 1, k1, psso.
Patt 5 rows. Rep these 6 rows once more.
Next row: Patt to last 2 sts, sl 1, k1, psso.
[30 (34) sts.]
Work 9 rows straight. Bind off.

RIGHT FRONT

With US 9 (5½ mm) needles and A, cast on
38 (46) sts and work 10 rows in 2x2 rib as
given for Back inc 2 (dec 1) st evenly on last
row. [40 (45) sts.]
Change to US 10½ (6½ mm) needles. Cont in
patt as follows:
Row 1: Right side. K16 (18) D, k16 (18) B,
k8 (9) A.
Work a further 33 (35) rows as set.
Row 35 (37): K16 (18) A, k16 (18) D,
k8 (9) C.
Work a further 33 (35) rows as set.
Rep rows 1 to 34 (36), then rows 35 (37) to
52 (54) once, ending with a WS row.
[120 (126) rows.]

Shape front slope

Next row: Place a marker. K2tog, patt to end.
Complete as given for Left Front, reversing
shapings.

RIGHT SLEEVE

With US 9 (5½ mm) needles and A, cast on 58 (62) sts and work 18 cm (7 in) in 2x2 rib as given for Back ending with a WS row.

Dec row: Rib 1 (5), *rib 2tog, rib 4 (5); rep from * 9 (7) times, rib 2tog, rib 1 (6). [48 (54) sts.]

Change to US 10½ (6½ mm) needles. ***

Cont in patt as follows:

Row 1: RS. K8 (9) A, k16 (18) B, k16 (18) C, k8 (9) D.

Cont as now set inc 1 st at each end of every 4th row 2 times [52 (58) sts], then every 6th row 4 times. [60 (66) sts.] Work 1 (3) row(s). [34 (36) rows.]

Row 35 (37): K14 (15) C, k16 (18) D, k16 (18) B, k14 (15) A.

Cont as now set inc 1 st at each end of the foll 5th (3rd) row, then every 6th row 3 times. [68 (74) sts.] Work 3 (5) rows straight.

Shape top

Work 7 rows dec 1 st at each end of every row. [54 (60) sts.] Bind off.

LEFT SLEEVE

Work as given for Right Sleeve to ***.

Cont in patt as follows:

Row 1: RS. K8 (9) D, k16 (18) C, k16 (18) B, k8 (9) A.

Cont as now set inc 1 st at each end of every 4th row 2 times [52 (58) sts], then every 6th

row 4 times. [60 (66) sts.]

Work 1 (3) rows. [34 (36) rows.]

Row 35 (37): K14 (15) A, k16 (18) B, k16 (18) D, k14 (15) C.

Complete as given for Right Sleeve.

BUTTON BAND AND COLLAR

Join shoulders.

With US 9 (5½ mm) needles and A, cast on 10 sts and work in 2x2 rib as given for Back until piece is long enough, when slightly stretched, to fit up Left Front to marker **, ending with a WS row. Mark end of last row with a colored thread.

Shape collar

Next row: Cast on 62 (66) sts, *p2, k2; rep from * to end. Rep this row. [72 (76) sts.]

Cont in rib as set until Collar measures 3 in (8 cm) from cast-on edge.

Change to US 10½ (6½ mm) needles and work a further 2½ in (6 cm) in rib as set. Bind off in rib.

Matching markers, sew Band to Left Front, then sew Collar neatly in place to center back of neck.

Mark the positions of 4 toggles on Band, the first to come 11 (11¾) in (28 (30.5) cm) up from cast-on edge, the last ¾ in (2 cm) down from marker, and the remainder spaced evenly between.

VARIATION: HAT WITH BRIM

To make this hat, you will need 2 × 50 g balls of Rowan Big Wool Tuft in Frosty 055. With US 36 (20 mm) needles cast on 28 sts. Cont in st st beg with a knit row until the hat measures 8 in (20 cm) from beg, ending with a WS row.

Shape crown

Work as for hat with earflaps.

TO FINISH

Break yarn and thread through sts, pull up tightly, and secure. Sew back seam, reversing seam on hat on the last 2½ in (6 cm) for brim. Press as instructions given on yarn label.

Work in rev st st, beg with a purl row, for 4 in (10 cm). Change to US 36 (20 mm) needles. Cont in rev st st until collar measures 8 in (20 cm) from beg. Knit 4 rows. Bind off loosely. Join left side and collar seam, reversing collar seam for turn-back. Along lower edge, tie in fringes that are about 4¾ in (12 cm) long, made with double yarn and spaced 3 sts apart.

TO FINISH

Press as instructions given on yarn label. Join right seam.

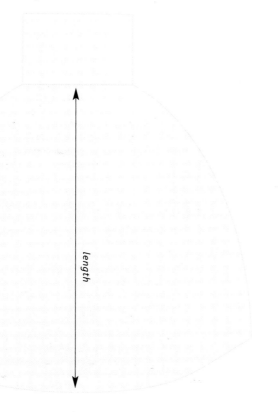

length

HAT WITH EARFLAPS

RIGHT EARFLAP

With US 36 (20 mm) needles cast on 5 sts. Cont in st st.
Row 1: Knit.
Row 2: Purl inc 1 st at both ends of row.
Row 3: Knit. **.
Row 4: Purl inc 1 st at end of row only. [8 sts.] Work 2 rows and leave sts on a st holder.

LEFT EARFLAP

Work as given for Right Earflap side to **.
Row 4: Purl inc 1 st at beg of row only. [8 sts.]

BODY OF HAT

With US 36 (20 mm) needles cast on 2 sts, knit across 8 sts from one ear flap, cast on 8 sts, knit across 8 sts from second ear flap, cast on 2 sts. [28 sts.]
Cont in st st beg with a purl row until main body of hat measures 6 in (15 cm) from cast-on edge, ending with a WS row.

Shape crown

Row 1: K1, (k2tog, k2) 6 times, k2tog, k1. [21 sts.]
Row 2: Purl.
Row 3: K1, (k2tog, k1) 6 times, k2tog. [14 sts.]
Row 4: Purl.
Row 5: (K2tog) 7 times. [7 sts.]

Luxuriously soft-to-the-touch, this oversized wrap can be knitted in an evening! Worked in a stockinette stitch using fat needles, the wrap has colorful texture that adds fashionable appeal and easy wearability.

THROW-OVER WRAP

★☆☆ BEGINNER

This project couldn't be simpler. The bulky yarn and large needles mean that it can be completed in a very short amount of time.

MEASUREMENTS
Actual width
50 in (127 cm)
Actual length (excluding fringing)
30¾ in (78 cm)

MATERIALS
- 18 × 100 g balls of Rowan Biggy in 246
- Pair each of US 19 (15 mm) and US 36 (20 mm) needles

GAUGE
5½ sts and 7 rows to 4 in (10 cm) measured over stockinette stitch using 20 mm needles.

ABBREVIATIONS
See page 10.

WRAP

LEFT SIDE
With US 19 (15 mm) needles, cast on 32 sts.
Knit 5 rows for hem.
Next row: WS. K2, purl to last 2 sts, k2.
Next row: Knit.
These 2 rows form the patt and are repeated throughout. **
Cont in patt until work measures 30¾ in (78 cm) from beg, ending with a RS row.
Next row: Cast on 3 sts for back neck, knit across these 3 sts, k2 then purl to last 2 sts, k2. [35 sts.]

Next row: Knit.
Next row: Purl to last 2 sts, k2.
Rep the last 2 rows until back measures same as front to top of hem, ending with a RS row. Knit 3 rows. Bind off knitwise.

RIGHT SIDE
Work as given for Left Side to **.
Cont in patt until work measures 30¾ in (78 cm) from beg, ending with a WS row.
Next row: Cast on 3 sts for back neck, purl across these 3 sts, purl 2, then knit to end. [35 sts.]
Next row: K2, purl to end.
Next row: Knit.
Rep the last 2 rows until back measures same as front to top of hem, ending with a RS row. Knit 3 rows. Bind off knitwise.

TO FINISH
Join center back seam neatly.
For each tassel, cut 3 lengths of yarn each 9¾ in (25 cm) long and tie in evenly along lower edges (see Making Tassels, page 13).

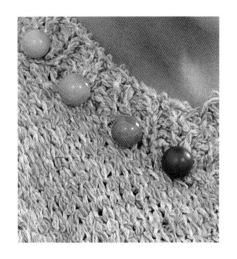

CASUAL

Casual elegance for everyday dressing: what could be easier to wear? These knitted cardigans, sweaters, and tops are gorgeously casual yet big on style, with simple stitch patterns and luxurious yarns. From the sweater with ruffled edges in a textured cotton yarn to the striped sleeveless top worked in a chenille yarn with its velvety pile, these are all wonderful to wear. All the patterns are easy to knit and some are ideal for the complete beginner – there is something here to suit everyone.

Dress up any outfit with this cardigan worked in stockinette stitch. Its striped feather-and-fan border pattern is knit simply by increasing and decreasing stitches at regular intervals. The cardigan is tied around the waist with ribbon and has coordinating ribbon on the cuffs.

CARDIGAN WITH RIBBON TIES

★★☆ MEDIUM

The challenging part of this project is in the zigzag design.

MEASUREMENTS
To fit bust
32–34	36–38	40–42	in
81–86	91–97	102–107	cm

Actual width
36	40	44½	in
91	102	113	cm

Actual length (to lowest hem point)
24½	25½	26¾	in
62	65	68	cm

Actual sleeve seam (to lowest cuff point)
19¼	20	20	in
49	51	51	cm

In the instructions, figures are given for the smallest size first; larger sizes follow in parentheses. Where only one set of figures is given, this applies to all sizes.

MATERIALS
- 10 (11:12) × 50 g balls of Rowan Wool Cotton in Poster Blue 948 (A)
- 1 × 50 g ball of Rowan Wool Cotton in Antique 900 (B)
- 1 × 50 g ball of Rowan Wool Cotton in French Navy 909 (C)
- Pair each of US 3 (3¼ mm) and US 6 (4 mm) needles
- Stitch holder
- Ribbon for waist and cuffs
- 9 buttons

GAUGE
22 sts and 30 rows to 4 in (10 cm) measured over stockinette stitch using US 6 (4 mm) needles.

ABBREVIATIONS
See page 10.

CARDIGAN

BACK
With US 6 (4 mm) needles and A, cast on 128 (146:164) sts and purl 3 rows.
Cont in patt as follows:
Row 1: WS. With A, purl.
Row 2: With A, k1, inc in next st (by knitting into front and back of st), k6, sl 1, k1, psso, k2tog, k6, *inc in each of next 2 sts, k6, sl 1, k1, psso, k2tog, k6; rep from * to last 2 sts, inc in next st, k1.
Row 3: With A, purl.
Row 4: As row 2.
Work 3 more rows in A, 4 rows in B, 2 rows in C, 2 rows in A as now set.
Row 16 (dec row): RS. With A, k1, inc in next st, k2, k2tog, k2, sl 1, k1, psso, (k2tog, k2) twice; *inc in each of next 2 sts, k2, k2tog, k2, sl 1, k1, psso, (k2tog, k2) twice; rep from * to last 2 sts, inc in next st, k1. [114 (130:146) sts.]
Row 17 and 19: With A, purl.
Row 18: With A, k1, inc in next st, k5, sl 1, k1, psso, k2tog, k5, *inc in each of next 2 sts,

k5, sl 1, k1, psso, k2tog, k5; rep from * to last 2 sts, inc in next st, k1.

Work 3 more rows in A, 4 rows in B, 2 rows in C, 2 rows in A as now set.

Row 30 (dec row): RS. With A, k1, inc in next st, k1, k2tog, k2, sl 1, k1, psso, k2tog, k1, k2tog, k2, *inc in each of next 2 sts, k1, k2tog, k2, sl 1, k1, psso, k2tog, k1, k2tog, k2; rep from * to last 2 sts, inc in next st, k1. [100 (114:128) sts.]

Row 31: With A, purl.

Row 32: With A, k1, inc in next st, k4, sl 1, k1, psso, k2tog, k4, * inc in each of next 2 sts, k4, sl 1, k1, psso, k2tog, k4; rep from * to last 2 sts, inc in next st, k1.

Work 15 more rows in A as now set (47 patt rows have been worked).

Eyelet and dec row: With A, k1, (k2tog, yon) twice, [(k2tog, yon) twice, k3tog, yon] 12 (14:16) times, (k2tog, yon) 5 times, k1. [88 (100:112) sts.]

Next row: With A, purl.

Cont in st st and A, beg with a knit row, at the same time inc 1 st at each end of the foll 7th (7th:9th) row, then every 8th (9th:9th) row 5 times [100 (112:124) sts], then cont straight until work measures 8½ (9:9½) in (22 (23:24) cm) from top of eyelet row, ending with a WS row.

Shape armholes

Bind off 6 (7:9) sts at beg of the next 2 rows [88 (98:106) sts], then dec 1 st at each end of the next 5 (5:7) rows, then on the 0 (2:2) foll alt rows. [78 (84:88) sts.] Cont straight until armhole measures 7½ (8¼:9) in (19 (21:23) cm) from beg of shaping, ending with a WS row.

Shape shoulders and back neck

Bind off 6 sts at beg of the next row, knit until there are 22 (24:25) sts on RH needle after bind off, turn, and leave rem sts on a st holder. Work on these sts for the first side. Dec 1 st at neck edge on next row. Bind off 6 (6:7) sts for shoulder on next row and dec 1 st at neck edge. Dec 1 st at neck edge on next row. Bind off 6 (7:7) sts at shoulder on next row and dec 1 st at neck edge. Work 1 row. Bind off rem 6 (7:7) sts. With RS facing, rejoin yarn and bind off center 22 (24:26) sts, knit to end. Complete this side to match the first side, reversing shapings.

LEFT FRONT

With Us 6 (4 mm) needles and A, cast on 65 (74:83) sts and purl 3 rows.

Cont in patt as follows:

1st and 3rd sizes

Row 1: WS. With A, purl.

Row 2: With A, k1, inc in next st, k6, sl 1, k1, psso, k2tog, k6, *inc in each of the next 2 sts, k6, sl 1, k1, psso, k2tog, k6; rep from * to last 11 sts, inc in each of the next 2 sts, k6, sl 1, k1, psso, k1.

2nd size

As given for Back.

All sizes

Cont as now set and in same stripe sequence as Back.

1st and 3rd sizes

Row 16 (dec row): Work in same way as given for Back to the last 11 sts, inc in each of next 2 sts, k2, k2tog, k2, sl 1, k1, psso, k1. [58 (74) sts.]

Row 30 (dec row): Work in same way as given for Back to the last 10 sts, inc in each of the next 2 sts, k1, k2tog, k2, sl 1, k1, psso, k1. [51 (65) sts.]

2nd size

Row 16 (dec row): Work in same way as given for Back to the last 2 sts, k2. [66 sts.]

Row 30 (dec row): Work in same way as given for Back to the last 2 sts, k2. [58 sts.]

All sizes

Cont until all 47 patt rows have been worked.

Eyelet and dec row: With A, k1, [(k2tog, yo) twice, k3tog, yo] 7 (8:9) times, k1. [44 (50:56) sts.]

Next row: With A, purl. Cont in st st and A beg with a knit row, inc 1 st at side edge on the 7th (7th:9th) row, then every 8th (9th:9th) row 5 times [50 (56:62) sts], then work straight until Front measures same as Back to beg of armhole shaping, ending with a WS row.

Shape armhole and front edge

Bind off 6 (7:9) sts at beg of the next row, knit to the last 2 sts, k2tog. [43 (48:52) sts.] Purl 1 row. (Dec 1 st at each end of the next row, then 1 st at armhole edge on the next row) 2 (2:3) times. [37 (42:43) sts.] Dec 1 st at each end of the next row. [35 (40:41) sts.]

2nd and 3rd sizes

Dec 1 st at each end of the 2 foll alt rows. [36 (37) sts.]

All sizes

Keeping armhole edge straight, cont to dec 1 st at front edge on the 2 (0:0) foll alt rows, then every 4th row 9 (10:10) times [24 (26:27) sts], then work straight until Front measures same as Back to beg of shoulder shaping, ending with a WS row.

Shape shoulder

Bind off 6 sts at beg of the next row, 6 (6:7) sts on the foll alt row, 6 (7:7) sts on the foll alt row. Work 1 row. Bind off rem 6 (7:7) sts.

RIGHT FRONT

Work as given for Left Front, placing patt as follows:

1st and 3rd sizes

Row 1: With A, purl.

Row 2: With A, k1, k2tog, k6, *inc in each of the next 2 sts, k6, sl 1, k1, psso, k2tog, k6; rep from * to last 2 sts, inc in next st, k1.

2nd size

Work as given for Back.

All sizes

Complete as given for Left Front, reversing shapings.

SLEEVES (MAKE 2)

With US 6 (4 mm) needles and A, cast on 66 sts. Purl 3 rows.

Row 1: With A, purl.

Row 2: With A, k1, inc in next st, k5, sl 1, k1, psso, k2tog, k5, *inc in each of next 2 sts, k5, sl 1, k1, psso, k2tog, k5; rep from * to last 2 sts, inc in next st, k1.

Row 3: With A, purl.

Cont in patt as given for Back, but in stripe sequence as follows:

Work 4 more rows in A, 4 rows in B, 2 rows in C, 2 rows in A.

Row 16 (dec row): With A, k1, inc in next st, k1, k2tog, k2, sl 1, k1, psso, k2tog, k2, k2tog, k1, *inc in each of next 2 sts, k1, k2tog, k2, sl 1, k1, psso, k2tog, k2, k2tog, k1; rep from * to last 2 sts, inc in next st, k1. [58 sts.]

Row 17: With A, purl.

Row 18: With A, k1, inc in next st, k4, sl 1, k1, psso, k2tog, k4, *inc in each of next 2 sts, k4, sl 1, k1, psso, k2tog, k4; rep from * to last 2 sts, inc in next st, k1.

Work 3 more rows in A, 4 rows in B, 2 rows in C, 3 rows in A.

Dec row: With A, p1 (3:3), *p2tog, p4 (5:8); rep from * 9 (7:5) times, p2tog, p1 (4:3). [48 (50:52) sts.]

Eyelet row: K2 (1:2), *k2tog, yon; rep from * to last 2 (1:2) sts, k2 (1:2).

Next row: With A, purl.

Cont in A and st st beg with a knit row, at the same time inc 1 st at each end of every 5th row 16 (17:19) times. [80 (84:90) sts.] Cont straight until sleeve measures 13½ (14:14) in (34 (36:36) cm) from top of eyelet row, ending with a WS row.

Shape sleeve top

Bind off 6 (7:9) sts at beg of the next 2 rows [68 (70:72) sts], then dec 1 st at each end of the next 10 rows [48 (50:52) sts], then every 4th row 3 (4:5) times [42 (42:42) sts], then on the next 12 rows. [18 sts.] Bind off.

BUTTON BAND

With US 3 (3¼ mm) needles and A, cast on 7 sts. Cont in rib as follows:

Row 1: RS. K1, (k1b, p1) twice, k1b, k1.

Row 2: K1, (p1, k1b) 3 times.

Cont in rib as set until band (when slightly stretched) fits up left front to beg of front edge shaping, ending with a 2nd rib row.

Shape collar

Rib 3, k1, p1 into back of loop between st just knitted and next st, rib to end.

Work 3 rows without inc.

Rep the last 4 rows until there are 37 sts ending at straight edge (opposite side to incs). Bind off 10 sts, return st on RH needle to LH needle, recast on 10 sts using cable method (insert RH needle between first two sts on LH needle, yon, place loop onto LH needle).

Work straight until collar fits to center of back neck. Bind off ribwise.

Sl st into place.

Place markers for buttons, the first ¾ in (2 cm) up from cast-on edge, the last ¾ in (2 cm) down from beg of front edge shaping, and the remainder spaced evenly between.

BUTTONHOLE BAND

Work as given for Button Band, making buttonholes to correspond with markers on Button Band as follows:-

Row 1: RS. Rib 3, (yon) twice, k2tog-tbl, rib 2.

Row 2: Rib across row dropping one of the (yon) loops.

Complete as given for Button Band.

Shape collar

Rib to last 3 sts, p1 and k1 into back of loop between st just knitted and next st, p1, k1b, k1. [9 sts.]

TO FINISH

Press as instructions on yarn label.

Join shoulders. Join collar seam at center of back neck, then sew to back neck. Sew sleeve tops into armholes, then join side and sleeve seams. Thread ribbon through eyelet holes on waist and sleeves.

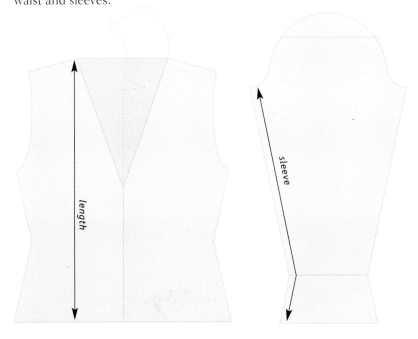

Shape shoulders and back neck

Bind off 3 (4:4:4:4:4) sts at beg of the next row, knit until there are 11 (11:11:11:12:13) sts on right hand needle after bind offs, turn and work on these sts for first side. Leave rem sts on a st holder.

Work 3 rows dec 1 st at neck edge on each row and casting off 4 (4:4:4:4:5) sts for shoulder on the 2nd row. Bind off rem 4 (4:4:4:5:5) sts.

With RS facing, leave the center 7 (8:9:10:9:10) sts on a st holder, rejoin yarn, and knit rem 14 (15:15:15:16:17) sts. Complete this side to match first side, reversing shapings.

LEFT FRONT

With US 10½ (6½ mm) needles cast on 21 (23:25:27:27:29) sts and work 6 rows in rib as given for Back inc 1 (1:0:0:1:1) sts in center on last row. [22 (24:25:27:28:30) sts.]

Change to US 11 (8 mm) needles. Cont in st st beg with a knit row shaping side by dec 1 st at RH edge on the 5th, then every 6th row 3 times [18 (20:21:23:24:26) sts], then inc 1 st at same edge on the foll 8th, then every 6th row 3 times. [22 (24:25:27:28:30) sts.] Cont straight until Front measures same as Back to beg of armhole shaping, ending with a WS row.

Shape armhole

Bind off 3 (3:4:4:5:5) sts at beg of the next row [19 (21:21:23:23:25) sts], then dec 1 st at same edge on the 2 (2:2:3:3:3) foll alt rows. [17 (19:19:20:20:22) sts.] Cont straight until work measures 13 rows shorter than Back to beg of shoulder shaping, ending with a RS row.

Shape neck

Bind off 3 (4:4:5:4:5) sts at beg of the next row [14 (15:15:15:16:17) sts], then dec 1 st at neck edge on the 3 foll alt rows. Work 6 rows straight, ending at armhole edge. [11 (12:12:12:13:14) sts.]

Shape shoulder

Bind off 3 (4:4:4:4:4) sts at beg of the next row, 4 (4:4:4:4:5) sts on the foll alt row. Work 1 row. Bind off rem 4 (4:4:4:5:5) sts.

RIGHT FRONT

Work as given for Left Front, reversing shapings.

SLEEVES (MAKE 2)

With US 10½ (6½ mm) needles, cast on 21 (21:23:23:25:25) sts and work 6 rows in rib as given for Back.

Change to US 11 (8 mm) needles. Cont in st st beg with a knit row, at the same time inc 1 st at each end of the 7th (5th:5th:5th:5th:5th) row, then every 8th (6th:6th:6th:6th:6th) row 6 (1:1:1:5:7) times [35 (25:27:27:37:41) sts], then every 0 (8th:8th:8th:8th:8th) row 0 (6:6:6:3:2) times. [35 (37:39:39:43:45) sts.] Cont straight until Sleeve measures 17 (18:18: 18:18:18½) in (43 (46:46:46:46:47) cm) from beg, ending with a WS row.

Shape sleeve top
Bind off 3 (3:4:4:5:5) sts at beg of the next 2 rows [29 (31:31:31:33:35) sts], then dec 1 st at each end of the next and 7 (7:8:8:9:9) foll alt rows [13 (15:13:13:13:15) sts], then on the next 3 rows. [7 (9:7:7:7:9) sts.] Bind off.

NECKBAND
Join shoulders.
With RS facing and US 10½ (6½ mm) needles, knit up 17 (18:18:19:19:20) sts from right front neck edge, 3 sts from right back neck, working across st holder for back neck, k7 (8:9:10:9:10) sts from back neck dec 0 (1:0:1:0:1) sts in center of these sts, pick up and knit 3 sts from left back neck and 17 (18:18:19:19:20) sts down left front neck. [47 (49:51:53:53:55) sts.] Work 5 rows in rib as given for Back. Bind off in rib.

BUTTON BAND
With US 10½ (6½ mm) needles cast on 6 sts and cont in rib as follows:
Row 1: RS. Sl 1, (k1, p1) twice, k1b.
Rep this row until band fits up left front to top of neckband. Bind off in rib. Sew in place.

Mark the position of 7 buttons, the first ¾ in (1.5 cm) up from cast-on edge, the last ¾ in (1.5cm) down from top of neckband and the remainder spaced evenly between.

BUTTONHOLE BAND
With US 10½ (6½ mm) needles cast on 6 sts and cont in rib as button band, making buttonholes to correspond with markers as follows:
Buttonhole row 1: RS. Sl 1, k1, bind off next st, rib to end.
Buttonhole row 2: In rib casting on over bind off st on previous row.

TO FINISH
Sew sleeve heads into armholes, then join side and sleeve seams. Sew on buttons. Sew on beads.

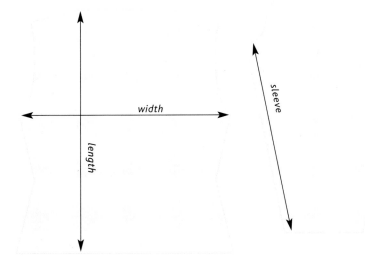

Cont as follows:

Row 1: K19 (21:23:25:27), p1, k1b, (p2, k2) 7 times, p1, k1b, p1, k19 (21:23:25:27).

Row 2: P19 (21:23:25:27), k1, p1, k2, (p2, k2) 6 times, p2, k1, p1, k1, p19 (21:23:25:27).

Row 3: K19 (21:23:25:27), p1, k1b, (k2, p2) 7 times, k1, k1b, p1, k19 (21:23:25:27).

Row 4: P19 (21:23:25:27), k1, p3, (k2, p2) 7 times, k1, p19 (21:23:25:27).

These 4 rows form the patt. Cont in patt until work measures 13½ in (34 cm) from beg, ending with a WS row.

Shape armholes

Bind off 3 (3:4:4:5) sts at beg of the next 2 rows [65 (69:71:75:77) sts], then dec 1 st at each end of the 5 (5:6:6:7) foll alt rows. [55 (59:59:63:63) sts.]
Cont straight in patt until armhole measures 6 (6:6¼:6½:7) in (15 (15:16:17:18) cm) from beg of shaping, ending with a WS row.

Shape neck

K18 (19:19:20:20), turn, and leave rem sts on a st holder, work on these sts for first side. Work 10 rows, dec 1 st at neck edge on every row. Work 1 row. Bind off rem 8 (9:9:10:10) sts.
With RS facing, slip the center 19 (21:21:23:23) sts on a st holder, rejoin yarn, and patt to end. Complete this side to match first side, reversing shapings.

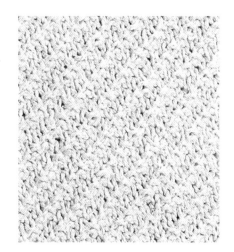

SLEEVES (MAKE 2)

With US 8 (5 mm) needles cast on
87 (87:99:99:111) sts and work the 18 rows of
bell edge as given for Back.
[31 (31:35:35:39) sts.]

Cont in st st beg with a knit row, at the same
time inc 1 st at each end of the 3rd, then
every 4th row 3 times, then every 8th row
8 (9:9:9:9) times. [55 (57:61:61:65) sts.]

Cont straight until sleeve measures
17½ (18½:18½:18½:18½) in (44 (47:47:47:47) cm)
from beg, ending with a WS row.

Shape sleeve top

Bind off 3 (3:4:4:5) sts at beg of the next
2 rows [49 (51:53:53:55) sts], then dec 1 st at
each end of the next and 8 (7:8:8:11) foll alt
rows [31 (35:35:35:31) sts], then on the next
9 (11:11:11:9) rows. Bind off rem 13 sts.

NECKBAND

Join left shoulder.

With US 8 (5 mm) needles, knit up 9 sts
down right back neck, knit across 19 (21:21:
23:23) sts from st holder, knit up 9 sts up left
back neck, 9 sts down left front neck, knit
across 19 (21:21:23:23) sts from st holder,
pick up and knit 9 sts up right front neck.
[74 (78:78:82:82) sts.] Knit 1 row. Bind off.

TO FINISH

Join right shoulder.
Sew sleeve tops into armholes, then join
side and sleeve seams.

HELPFUL HINT

*When measuring your
work, lay the pieces out
on a flat surface and
smooth out, without
stretching. This will
guarantee accurate
measurements.*

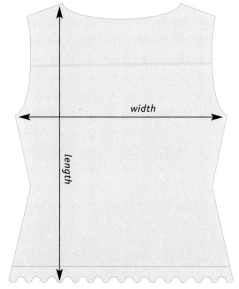

Row 9: K3 (4:3:5:4:6), p1, *k7, p1, k4, p1; rep from * to last 11 (12:11:13:12:14) sts, k7, p1, k3 (4:3:5:4:6).

Row 11: K3 (4:3:5:4:6), p1, *sl 1, k1, psso, k3, k2tog, p1, k4, p1; rep from * to last 11 (12:11:13:12:14) sts, sl 1, k1, psso, k3, k2tog, p1, k3 (4:3:5:4:6).

Row 13: K3 (4:3:5:4:6), p1, *sl 1, k1, psso, k1, k2tog, p1, k4, p1; rep from * to last 9 (10:9:11:10:12) sts, sl 1, k1, psso, k1, k2tog, p1, k3 (4:3:5:4:6).

Row 15: K3 (4:3:5:4:6), p1, *sl 1, k2tog, psso, p1, k4, p1; rep from * to last 7 (8:7:9:8:10) sts, sl 1, k2tog, psso, p1, k3 (4:3:5:4:6).

Row 16: As Row 4.

Cont in st st beg with a knit row until work measures 12 (12:12:12¼:12¼:12¼) in (30 (30:30:31:31:31) cm) from beg, ending with a WS row. **

Shape raglan

Bind off 3 (3:3:3:4:4) sts at beg of the next 2 rows. [52 (54:59:63:66:70) sts.]

1st, 2nd, 3rd, and 4th sizes only

Work 12 (12:8:4) rows dec 1 st at both ends of the next and every foll 4th (4th:4th:0th) row. [46 (48:55:61) sts.]

All sizes

Work 12 (14:20:24:28:32) rows dec 1 st at both ends of the next and every foll alt row, 34 (34:35:37:38:38) sts. Bind off rem sts.

FRONT

Work as given for Back to **.

Shape raglan

Bind off 3 (3:3:3:4:4) sts at beg of the next 2 rows. [52 (54:59:63:66:70) sts.]

1st, 2nd, 3rd and 4th sizes only

Work 12 (12:8:4) rows dec 1 st at both ends of the next and every foll 4th (4th:4th:0th) row. [46 (48:55:61) sts.]

All sizes

Work 4 (6:12:16:20:24) rows dec 1 st at both ends of the next and every foll alt row. [42 (42:43:45:46:46) sts.]

Shape neck

Next row: K2tog, k7, turn, and leave rem 33 (33:34:36:37:37) sts on a st holder. Working on these 8 sts only proceed as follows:

Next row: Purl.

Work 5 rows dec 1 st at both ends of the next and every foll alt row. [2 sts.]

Next row: P2tog.

Fasten off.

With RS facing, rejoin yarn to rem 33 (33:34:36:37:37) sts, bind off 24 (24:25:27:28:28) sts, knit to last 2 sts, k2tog. [8 sts.] Complete to match first side of neck.

SLEEVES (MAKE 2)

Using US 9 (5½ mm) needles cast on

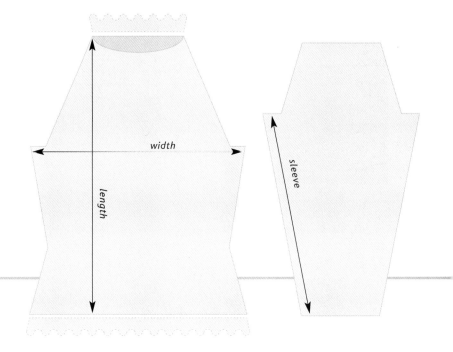

38 (38:42:42:46:46) sts, work 2 in (5 cm) in rib as follows, ending with a WS row:

Row 1: RS. *K2, p2; rep from * to last 2 sts, k2.

Row 2: *P2, k2; rep from * to last 2 sts, p2. Change to US 10½ (6½ mm) needles. Cont in st st beg with a knit row, inc 1 st at both ends of the 5th then each and every foll 6th (6th:6th: 6th:7th:7th) row to 50 (50:54:54:58:58) sts. Work straight until sleeve measures 9¾ (10¾:10¾:10¾:11:11) in (25 (27:27:27:28:28) cm) or length required, ending with a WS row.

Shape raglan

Bind off 3 (3:3:3:4:4) sts at beg of the next 2 rows. [44 (44:48:48:50:50) sts.]
Work 8 (12:8:8:4:12) rows dec 1 st at both ends of the next and every foll 4th (4th:4th: 4th:0th:4th) row. [40 (38:44:44:48:44) sts.]
Work 16 (14:20:20:24:20) rows dec 1 st at both ends of the next and every foll alt row. Bind off rem 24 sts.

NECKBAND

With US 9 (5½ mm) needles and using the thumb method, cast on 211 (211:211:222:222:222) sts.

Row 1: RS. Purl.

Row 2: K2, *k1, slip this st back onto LH needle, lift the next 8 sts on LH needle over this st and off needle, (yf) twice, knit the first st again, k2; rep from * to end.

Row 3: K1, *p2tog, drop loop of 2 sts made in previous row and (k1, k1b) twice, into it, p1; rep from * to last st, k1. ***
[116 (116:116:122:122:122) sts.]
Knit 2 rows.

Eyelet row: K4 (4:4:2:2:2), * yf, k2tog, k2; rep from * to end.
Purl 3 rows. Bind off knitwise.

LOWER BORDER

With US 9 (5½ mm) circular needle and using the thumb method, cast on 211 (222:233:244:255:266) sts and work as given for Neckband to ***.
[116 (122:128:134:140:146) sts.]
Knit 4 rows. Bind off knitwise.

TO FINISH

Join raglans, then side and sleeve seams. Beginning at center back, sew Neckband to neck edge and Lower Border to lower edge beginning at side seam. Join short ends. Thread ribbon in and out of eyelets on neckband and tie in a bow at center of front neck. Pin out garment to the measurement given on page 96. Cover with damp cloths and leave until dry.

Shape armholes

Bind off 4 (4:5:5:6) sts at beg of the next
2 rows [53 (57:59:63:65) sts], then dec 1 st
at both ends of the next 4 rows
[45 (49:51:55:57) sts], then on the 3 foll alt
rows. [39 (43:45:49:51) sts.]
Cont straight in patt until armhole measures
8 (8¼:8½:9:9½) in (20 (21:22:23:24) cm) from
beg, ending with a WS row.

Shape shoulders and back of neck

Bind off 3 (4:4:5:5) sts at beg of the next row,
knit until there are 8 (9:9:10:10) sts on RH
needle after bind-off. Work on these sts for
first side. Bind off 4 sts at neck edge on next
row. Bind off rem 4 (5:5:6:6) sts.
With RS facing, slip the center
17 (17:19:19:21) sts on a st holder, rejoin yarn
and knit to end. Complete as given for first
side, reversing shapings.

FRONT

Work as given for Back to **.

Shape armholes and divide for V-neck

Bind off 4 (4:5:5:6) sts at beg of the next row,
knit until there are 26 (28:29:31:32) sts on
RH needle after bind-off. Turn and work on
these sts for first side.

Dec 1 st at beg of the next row. Work 10 rows dec 1 st at neck edge every 4th row 2 times, at the same time, dec 1 st at armhole edge on the next 4 rows and 3 foll alt rows. [16 (18:19:21:22) sts.]

Keeping armhole edge straight, cont to dec 1 st at neck edge on every 4th row to 7 (9:9:11:11) sts, then work straight until Front matches Back to beg of shoulder shaping, ending with a WS row.

Shape shoulder

Bind off 3 (4:4:5:5) sts at beg of the next row. Work 1 row. Bind off rem 4 (5:5:6:6) sts. With RS facing, slip the center st onto a safety pin (this marks the st), rejoin yarn, and knit to end. Complete this side to match first side, reversing shapings.

NECKBAND

Join left shoulder. With RS facing, US 6 (4 mm) needles and A, pick up and knit 3 sts from right back neck, knit across 17 (17:19:19:21) sts from back neck st holder, dec 1 st in center of these sts, pick up and knit 3 sts from left back neck, 35 (37:39:41: 43) sts down left front neck, knit marked st, pick up and knit 35 (37:39:41:43) sts up right front neck. [93 (97:103:107:113) sts.]

Next row: Beg with a 2nd rib row, rib to within 2 sts of marked st, p2tog, p1, p2tog-tbl, rib rem 55 (57:61:63:67) sts.

Next row: Rib to within 2 sts of marked st, k2tog-tbl, k1b, k2tog, rib to end. Rib 3 more rows, dec either side of marked st as set. [83 (87:93:97:103) sts.] Bind off ribwise, dec as before.

ARMBANDS (MAKE 2)

Join right shoulder and neckband. With RS facing, US 6 (4 mm) needles and A, pick up and knit 81 (85:89:93:97) sts evenly along one armhole edge. Beg with a 2nd rib row, rib 5 rows. Bind off ribwise.

TO FINISH

Join side seams.

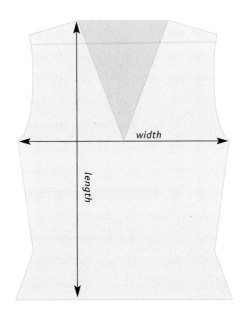

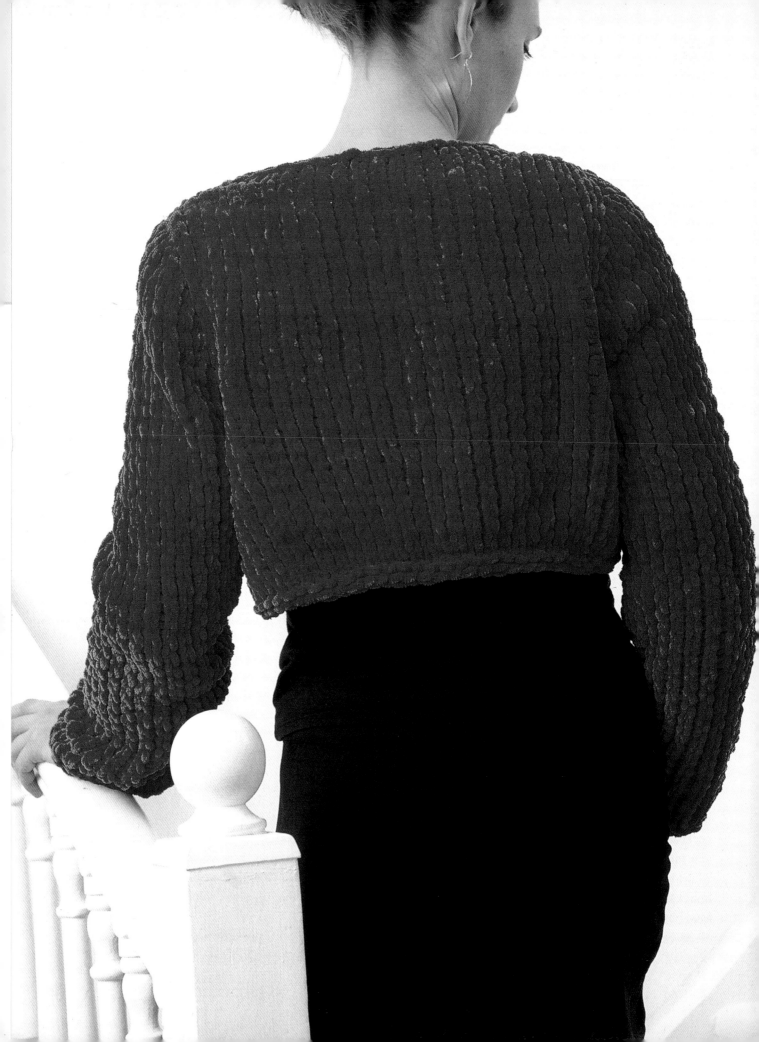

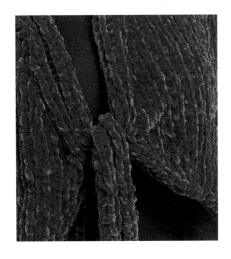

GLAMOROUS

This chapter features elegant items perfect for evenings out. Fortunately, you don't have to be an expert to create them. They are really versatile to wear – you can relax in casual style or dress up for a more formal look. Wrap yourself in the cape teamed with the headband, or slip on the bolero if you need added warmth to keep out the night time chill. Both are worked in luxurious chenille yarn. Or try the beautiful textured wraparound cardigan with ties. Shimmer and look extra special in the fitted sweater with lace collar and cuffs, worked in a lurex yarn.

You will feel special when wearing this cape, worked in simple stockinette stitch. Ties at the front keep the cape snugly on shoulders, and a wide headband adds glamour and warmth.

CAPE AND HEADBAND

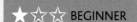
★ ☆ ☆ BEGINNER

Using large size needles and a thicker yarn means that this garment is really quick and easy to pick up and knit.

HELPFUL HINTS

- Always knit chenille yarns by taking the yarn from the 'outside' of the ball.
- To join in a new ball of chenille yarn, remove approximately 2 in (5 cm) of chenille from the end of the old and beginning of the new balls by drawing fibres between your thumbnail and index finger, leaving 2 in (5 cm) of core yarn exposed. Knot these core ends firmly together as close to the remaining chenille as possible and trim the ends.
- When sewing up garments knitted in chenille, use a plain yarn in a matching color.

MEASUREMENTS
To fit bust

32	34	36	38	40	42	in
81	86	91	97	102	107	cm

Actual width

51¼	54	56	59	61	63¾	in
130	137	142	150	155	162	cm

Actual length

14	14	14	15	15	15	in
35.5	35.5	35.5	38	38	38	cm

In the instructions, figures are given for the smallest size first; larger sizes follow in parentheses. Where only one set of figures is given, this applies to all sizes.

MATERIALS

- 5 (5:6:7:7) × 100 g balls of Sirdar Wow! in Imperial Purple 760
- Pair each of US 11 (8 mm) and US 10½ (6½ mm) needles

GAUGE

8 sts and 15 rows to 4 in (10 cm) measured over stockinette stitch, using US 10½ (6½ mm) needles.

ABBREVIATIONS

See page 10.

CAPE

BACK

With US 11 (8 mm) needles cast on 52 (55:57:60:62:65) sts.
Change to US 10½ (6½ mm) needles. Cont in st st beg with a knit row.
Work 6 rows, then dec 1 st at each end of the next, then every 10th row 2 times.
[46 (49:51:54:56:59) sts.]
Dec 1 st every 4th row 1 (1:1:2:2:2) times
[44 (47:49:50:52:55) sts], then on the 8 foll alt rows [28 (31:33:34:36:39) sts], then on the next row.
[26 (29:31:32:34:37) sts.]

Shape shoulders and back neck

Next row: K2tog, knit until there are 8 (9:10:10:11:12) sts on RH needle, turn, and leave rem sts on a st holder. Dec 1 st at each end of the next 2 rows. [4 (5:6:6:7:8) sts.] Bind off.

With RS facing, rejoin yarn to rem sts, bind off 8 (9:9:10:10:11) sts, and knit to last 2 sts, k2tog. Complete this side to match first side, reversing shapings.

LEFT FRONT

With US 11 (8 mm) needles cast on 14 (15:16:17:18:19) sts.

Change to US 10½ (6½ mm) needles. Cont in st st beg with a knit row.

Row 1: Knit.

Row 2: Cast on 2 sts, purl these 2 sts, then purl to end.

Work 4 rows inc 1 st at front edge on every row. [20 (21:22:23:24:25) sts.]

Row 7: Dec 1 st at side edge, inc 1 st at front edge.

Work 2 rows inc 1 st at front edge on every row. [22 (23:24:25:26:27) sts.]

Work 1 row.

Inc 1 st at front edge on the next row. [23 (24:25:26:27:28) sts.]

Work 5 rows straight, place a marker at front edge on last row.

Dec 1 st at side edge on next row.

Work 1 row.

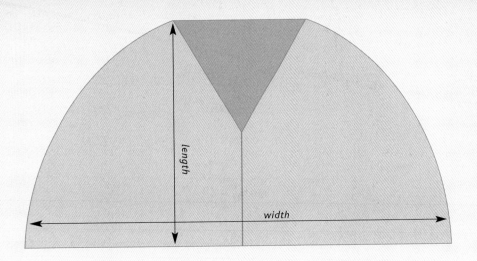

(Dec 1 st at front edge on the next row, work 3 rows straight) twice.
[20 (21:22:23:24:25) sts.]
Dec 1 st at each end of the next, then every 4th row 1 (1:1:3:3:3) times.
[16 (17:18:15:16:17) sts.]

1st, 2nd, and 3rd sizes only
Work 1 row.
Dec 1 st at side edge on the next row.
Work 1 row.
Dec 1 st at each end of the next row.
[13 (14:15) sts.]

All sizes
Keeping front edge straight, cont to dec 1 st at side edge on the 6 foll alt rows
[7 (8:9:9:10:11) sts], then on the next 3 rows.
[4 (5:6:6:7:8) sts.]
Work 1 row. Bind off.

RIGHT FRONT
Work as given for Left Front, reversing shapings.

FRONT BAND AND TIES (WORKED IN ONE PIECE)
Join side edges.
With US 10½ (6½ mm) needles cast on 5 sts.
Row 1: RS. K2 * P1, k1; rep from * to last st, k1.
Row 2: K1 * p1, k1; rep from * to end.
Cont in rib until piece measures 13½ in (34 cm), place a marker, then cont in rib until piece fits from marker on right front to marker on left front, work a further 13½ in (34 cm). Bind off.

TO FINISH
Sew side seams.
Attach ties to front edge between markers.

LOWER EDGE
With RS facing and US 10½ (6½ mm) needles, pick up and knit 34 (35:36:37:38:39) sts from tie round left front curve to side seam, 49 (52:54:57:59:62) sts along back, 34 (35:36:37:38:39) sts round right front curve to tie. [117 (122:126:131:135:140) sts.]
Knit 1 row. Change to US 11 (8 mm) needles and bind off loosely.

BOBBLE AND CORD (MAKE 4)
With US 10½ (6½ mm) needles, cast on 3 sts, inc in 1st st, k1, inc in last st, 5 sts, turn and purl, turn and k1, sl 1, k2tog, psso, k1, turn, p3tog. With rem st work a cord. Knit 4 rows. Fasten off. Attach two bobble and cords to each end of front ties.

HEADBAND

With US 10½ (6½ mm) needles, cast on 7 sts and work in rib as given for Front Band until piece reaches the desired length to fit around head. Bind off ribwise. Join seam.

Feel extra special in this lovely cardigan worked in stockinette stitch with an unusual ribbon yarn. The ruffled edge on the bodice and cuffs are worked in a cotton yarn adding extra femininity. The sweater is wrapped around the waist and secured with pretty knitted ties.

WRAPAROUND CARDIGAN WITH TIES

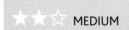 **MEDIUM**

The shaping at the front of the garment and the frilled edges require some knitting skill.

HELPFUL HINTS
- Use a firm back stitch when sewing the frill to the front edges to keep the garment in the correct shape, because the main yarn is stretchy.

MEASUREMENTS
To fit bust

32	34	36	38	40	in
81	86	91	97	102	cm

Actual width

32½	34¼	36½	39	40½	in
83	87	93	99	103	cm

Actual length

19	19¼	19½	20	20½	in
48	49	50	51	52	cm

Actual sleeve seam (excluding frill)

17	17	17½	17½	17½	in
43	43	44	44	44	cm

In the instructions, figures are given for the smallest size first; larger sizes follow in parentheses. Where only one set of figures is given, this applies to all sizes.

MATERIALS
- 9 (10:11:12:13) × 50 g balls of Rowan Cotton Braid in Renoir 353 (A)
- 2 (2:3:3:4) × 50 g balls of Rowan 4-ply Cotton in Zest 134 (B)
- Pair of US 11 (8 mm) needles
- US 3 (3¼ mm) long circular needle

GAUGE
10½ sts and 17 rows to 4 in (10 cm) measured over stockinette stitch using US 11 (8 mm) needles.

ABBREVIATIONS
See page 10.

CARDIGAN

BACK
With US 11 (8 mm) needles and A, cast on 38 (40:43:46:48) sts. Cont in st st beg with a knit row, at the same time, inc 1 st at both ends of the 9th, then every 10th row 2 times. [44 (46:49:52:54) sts.] Work a further 11 (13:13:15:15) rows straight, ending with a WS row.

Shape armholes
Bind off 3 (3:4:4:4) sts at beg of the next 2 rows [38 (40:41:44:46) sts], then dec 1 st at both ends of the next 4 rows. [30 (32:33:36:38) sts.] Work a further 28 (28:30:30:32) rows, ending with a WS row.

Shape shoulders
Bind off 4 sts at beg of the next 2 rows, then 3 (3:3:4:4) sts at beg of the next 2 rows. Bind off rem 16 (18:19:20:22) sts.

YARN INFORMATION

Rowan 4 Ply Cotton: 100% cotton. 182 yd/170 m per 1¾ oz (50 g) ball.

Rowan Biggy Print: 100% merino wool. 33 yd/30 m per 3½ oz (100 g) ball.

Rowan Big Wool: 100% merino wool. 87 yd/80 m per 3½ oz (100 g) ball.

Rowan Big Wool Tuft: 97% merino wool, 3% nylon. 27 yd/25 m per 1¾ oz (50 g) ball.

Rowan Chunky Cotton Chenille: 100% cotton. 153 yd/140 m per 3½ oz (100 g) ball.

Rowan Chunky Print: 100% wool. 110 yd/100 m per 3½ oz (100 g) ball.

Rowan Cork: 95% merino wool, 5% nylon. 120 yd/110 m per 1¾ oz (50 g) ball.

Rowan Cotton Braid: 68% cotton, 22% viscose, 10% linen. 55 yd/50 m per 1¾ oz (50 g) ball.

Rowan Cotton Glace: 100% cotton. 126 yd/115 m per 1¾ oz (50 g) ball.

Rowan Handknit DK Cotton: 100% cotton. 90 yd/85 m per 1¾ oz (50 g) ball.

Rowan Kidsilk Haze: 70% super kid mohair, 30% silk. 229 yd/210 m per 1 oz (25 g) ball.

Rowan Lurex Shimmer: 80% viscose, 20% polyester. 103 yd/95 m per 1 oz (25 g) ball.

Rowan Plaid: 42% merino wool, 30 % acrylic fibre, 28% superfine alpaca. 110 yd/100 m per 3½ oz (100 g) ball.

Rowan Polar: 60% pure new wool, 30% alpaca, 10% acrylic. 110 yd/100 m per 3½ oz (100 g) ball.

Rowan Ribbon Twist: 70% wool, 25% acrylic, 5% polyamide. 66 yd/60 m per 3½ oz (100 g) ball.

Rowan Summer Tweed: 79% silk, 30% cotton. 118 yd/108 m per 1¾ oz (50 g) ball.

Rowan Wool Cotton: 50% merino wool, 50% cotton. 124 yd/113 m per 1¾ oz (50 g) ball.

Rowan Yorkshire Tweed Aran: 100% pure new wool. 175 yd/160 m per 3½ oz (100 g) ball.

Rowan Yorkshire Tweed Chunky: 100% pure new wool. 110 yd/100 m per 3½ oz (100 g) ball.

Sirdar Bigga: 50% wool, 50% acrylic. 44 yd/40 m per 3½ oz (100 g) ball.

Sirdar Denim Chunky: 60% acrylic, 25% cotton, 15% wool. 170 yd/156 m per 3½ oz (100 g) ball.

Sirdar New Fizz: 72% nylon, 19% acrylic, 9% polyester. 82 yd/75 m per 1¾ oz (50 g) ball.

Sirdar Wow: 100% polyester. 63 yd/58 m per 3½ oz (100 g) ball.

Sirdar Yo-Yo: 74% acrylic, 14% wool, 12% polyester. 874 yd/800 m per 14 oz (400 g) ball.

SUPPLIERS AND USEFUL ADDRESSES

USA

Accordis Acrylic Fibers
15720 John J.Delaney Dr.
Suite 204
Charlotte, NC 28277-2747
www.courtelle.com

Berroco, Inc
Elmdale Rd.
Uxbridge, MA 01569
Tel: (508) 278-2527

Brown Sheep Co., INC.
100662 Country Rd. 16
Scottsbluff, NE 69361
Tel: (308) 635-2198

Cherry Tree Hill Yarn
52 Church St.
Barton, VT 05822
Tel: (802) 525-3311

Coats & Clark
Consumer Services
P.O. Box 12229
Greeneville, SC 29612-0224
Tel: (800) 648-1479
www.coatsandclark.com

Dale of Norway, Inc.
6W23390 Stonebridge Dr.,
Waukesha, WI 53186
Tel: (262) 544-1996

Elite Yarns
300 Jackson St.
Lowell, MA 01852
Tel: (978) 453-2837

Herrschners Inc.
2800 Hoover Rd.
Stevens Point, WI 54481
www.herrschners.com

JCA Inc.
35 Scales Lane
Townsend, MA 01469
Tel: (978) 597-3002

Knitting Fever Inc.
PO Box 502
Roosevelt
New York 11575
Tel: (516) 546 3600

√ Lion Brand Yarn Co.
34 West 15th St.
New York, NY 10011
Tel: (212) 243-8995

Personal Threads
8025 West Dodge Rd.
Omaha, NE 68114
Tel: (800) 3306-7733
www.personalthreads.com

√ Red Heart ® Yarns
Two Lakepointe Plaza
4135 So. Stream Blvd.
Charlotte, NC 28217
www.coatsandclark.com

Rowan USA/Westminster
  Fibers, Inc.
4 Townsend West, Unit 8
Nashua, NH 03063
Tel: (603) 886-5041
www.knitrowan.com

Solutia/Acrilan ® Fibers
320 Interstate N.
Pkwy.,suite 500
Atlanta, GA 30339
www.themartyarns.com

TMA Yarns
206 W.140th St.
Los Angeles, CA 90061

Trendsetter Yarns
16742 Stagg St.
Van Nuys, CA 91406
Tel: (818) 780-5497

Unique Kolours
23 North Bacton Hill Rd.
Malvern, PA 19355
Tel: (610) 280-7720

Yarns and ...
26440 Southfield Rd., LL 3
Lathrup Village,
MI 48076-4551
Tel: (800) 520-YARN
www.yarns-and.com

CANADA

Diamond Yarn of Canada Ltd.
155 Martin Ross Ave.
North York, ON M3J 2L9
Tel: (416) 736-6111
or
9697 St Laurent
Montreal, OC H3L 2N1
Tel: (514) 388-6188

S.R. Kertzer, Ltd
105A Winges Rd.
Woodbridge, ON L4L 6C2
Tel: (800) 263-2354
www.kertzer.com

Lily ®
320 Livingston Ave. S.
Listowel, ON N4W 3H3
Tel: (519) 291-3780

Patons ®
320 Livingston Ave.s.
Listowel, ON N4W 3H3
www.patonsyarns.com

INDEX

ACKNOWLEDGEMENTS

I would like to thank all those involved in the creation of this book, especially to Rosemary Wilkinson and Clare Sayer for their continued support and organization. Thank you to Sian Irvine for her lovely photographs, models Emma, Jo, Kat, Natalie, and Sarah and Isobel Gillan for her design.

Special thanks go to the pattern checker Marilyn Wilson. Also to David Rawson and Pauline Brown at Sirdar, and Linda Parkhouse and all at Rowan, who helped to sort out the yarn requirements. A huge thank you to both Sirdar and Rowan for producing such lovely yarns, which help to inspire all the garments I design. And where would I be without my loyal knitters, Margaret Craik, Helen Hawe, Thelma Seager, Irene Hall, and Christine D'Acunzo? They always amaze me with their speed and efficiency to turn garments around, even at the busiest times of the year.

I shall always be indebted to the magazines and spinners who commission my designs and who have now become special people in my life. Especially Elena Costella and Allison Stewart who work for the D C Thompson group of magazines and Margaret Maino and Beth Johnson from Creative Plus Publishing Ltd.

I have to thank my family for getting my interest in knitting going in the first place, and also for putting up with being surrounded by wool for all these years, and my artistic temperament!

A very special thank you to my daughter Sarah, who soon became proficient in the skill, and helped with the knitting in this book, and to Robert my son, because he's my son. I suppose they will always have this image of their mum with knitting needles and wool.